PITTWATER
PARADISE

PITTWATER
PARADISE

– to help plan your next trip !
Come back soon, love Kathryn + Lee.

Go there soon Dane
for a holiday! love Helen
+ Sam

Joan Lawrence

KINGSCLEAR BOOKS

KINGSCLEAR BOOKS PTY LTD
Suite 2, 77 Willoughby Road
Crows Nest 2065
Phone (02) 439 5093
Facsimile (02) 906 2036

Designed by Elaine Rushbrooke.
Edited by Vivien Encel.
Front cover photograph by Susan Wright.

© KINGSCLEAR BOOKS 1994
ISBN 0-908272-29-4

Acknowledgements

A number of people of Pittwater kindly supplied information and I would like to thank Carmine Sablatnig of Palm Beach Golf Club, Judy Walton of Aquatic Airways, Palm Beach, Mike Buesnel of Atlantis Divers, Palm Beach, Li Kershaw of Gonsalves Boatshed, Palm Beach, Carl and Caressa Gonsalves of Palm Beach, Peter Verrills of Palm Beach Ferries, Jimmy Goddard of Careel Bay Boat Services, Graeme Norman of the Royal Prince Alfred Yacht Club, Graham Chatfield of the Royal Motor Yacht Club, Bayview Golf Club, Loquat Valley Anglican Preparatory School, Bayview, Lennie Duck of Church Point Ferries, the Librarian, Pittwater High School, Vicky Jellis, Avalon Golf Club, Bev Sutton of Frenchs Forest and Evelyn Malloch of Newport. Also thanks to Jervis Sparks and Sue Gould for their special contribution.

Title page:
The peninsula had a
profusion of wildflowers. A
c.1930 memory of gathering
flannel flowers.

Contents

*A map of the general
Pittwater area.*

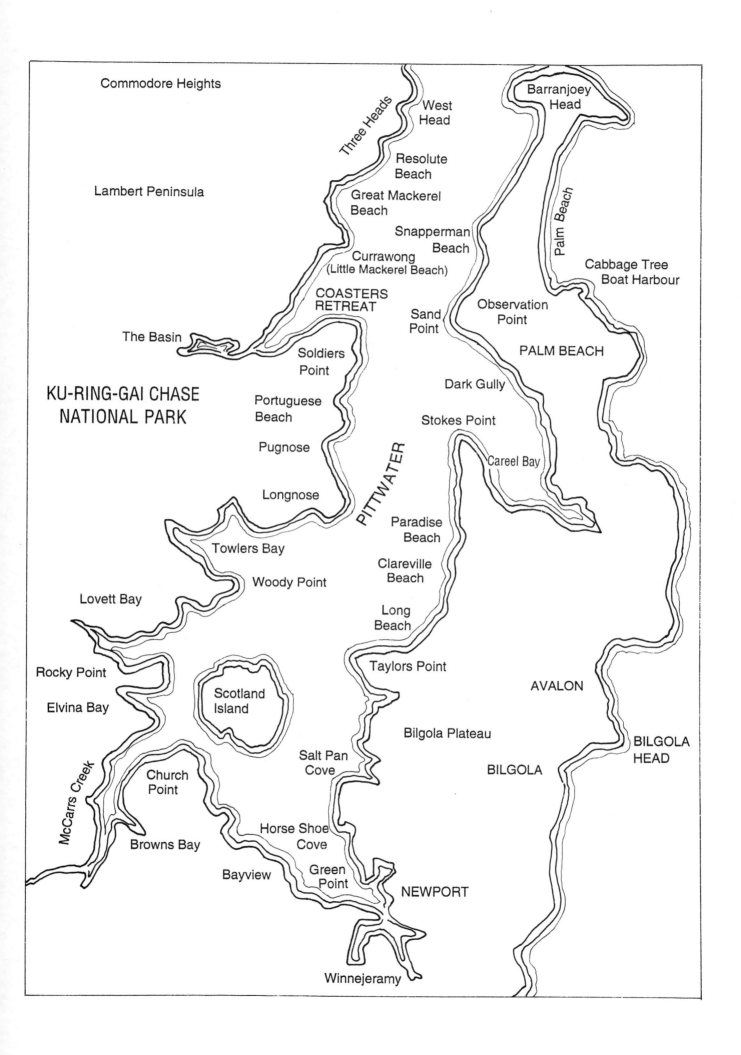

Pittwater Paradise

'but Pittwater's still a quiver of masts
and Broken Bay in the sun
is seamed with tacking arrowheads
and that's always gone on'.

Barrenjoey

Les Murray.

'The 2d of March I went with a long-boat and cutter to examine the broken land mentioned by Captain Cook, about eight miles (13 kms) to the northward of Port Jackson. We slept in the boat that night within a rocky point, in the north-west part of the bay (which is very extensive), as the natives, tho' very friendly, appeared to be numerous; and the next day, after passing a bar that had only water for small vessels, entered a very extensive branch, from which the ebb tide came out so strong that the boats could not row against it in the stream; and here was deep water. It appeared to end in several small branches, and in a large lagoon that we could not examine for want of time to search for a channel for the boats amongst the banks of sand and mud. Most of the land on the upper part of this branch was low and full of swamps. Pelicans and variety of birds were here seen in great numbers. Leaving this branch, which I called the north-west branch, we proceeded across the bay, and went into the south-west branch, which is very extensive, and from which a second branch runs to the westward, affording shelter for any number of ships, and as far as we examined there is water for the largest ships, having seven fathoms at the entrance, and deep water as you go up. But the almost continual rains prevented any kind of survey. Here the land is much higher than at Port Jackson, more rocky, and equally covered with timber, large trees growing on the summits of mountains that appear to be accessible to birds only.

'Immediately round the headland that forms the southern entrance into the bay there is a third branch, which I think the finest piece of water I ever saw, and which I honoured with the name of Pitt Water. It is, as well as the south-west branch, of sufficient extent to contain all the Navy of Great Britain, but has only eighteen feet at low water on a narrow bar which runs across the entrance. Within the bar there are from seven to fifteen fathom water. The land here is not so high as in the south-west branch, and there are some good situations where the land might be cultivated. We found small springs of water in most of the caves and saw three cascades falling from a height which the rains then rendered inaccessible. I returned to Port Jackson after being absent eight days in the boats. Some of the people feeling the effects of rain, which had been almost constant, prevented my returning by land, as I intended, in order to examine a part of the country which appeared open and free from timber.'

Thus wrote Captain Arthur Phillip, R.N., Governor of the new settlement at Sydney Cove, on 15 May 1788 to Lord Sydney, Secretary of the Home Department, the official responsible for colonial affairs.

Geology

Like Port Jackson and Botany Bay to the south the Pittwater estuary was formed by the drowning of an old river valley by the sea. Studies have revealed old river sediments and drainage patterns at the depths of Pittwater. In past geological times there may have been a broad peninsula. With a rise in the sea level some 16,000 to 6,000 years ago the area of Barrenjoey was converted from an isolated hill in rugged topography to an island and later to a 'tied island'. The area is joined to the mainland by the sand spit which formed later by a northward long shore drift up the coast and the creation of sand dunes which countered the high tide influence.[1] North Head in Port Jackson is a further example of a tied island.

Pittwater, with its wooded headlands of sandstone and modern suburbs where the houses perch on the hillsides or cling to precipitous cliffs, is a beautiful adjunct of Sydney.

Early Exploration

Governor Phillip named this newly discovered area north of the settlement at Sydney Cove Pitt Water for British Prime Minister, William Pitt the Younger (1759-1806). This powerful but shy and lonely man led Britain during the Napoleonic Wars and had considerable influence in strengthening the office of the British Prime Minister.

In the early years of the first settlement the northern peninsula was much explored. Governor Phillip, Lieutenant George Johnston, Lieutenant Cresswell of the Marines, Surgeon John White and six soldiers landed at Manly Cove on 22 August 1788 to walk overland to Broken Bay. They reached Pittwater but 'returned to the seashore, in order to examine the south part of the entrance into the bay' (Barrenjoey).[2] During this trek the abundance of flowers and shrubs were noted. The party returned overland to Manly to meet the boats to transport them back across Sydney Harbour. This journey must have been a strenuous walk through unknown virgin bush and the clothing of the party hardly suitable for 'bush bashing'. Early sketches such as that used as the frontispiece of Captain Hunter's journal show a marine in full uniform complete with gaiters and the other gentlemen clad in trousers, shirts, waistcoat and coats but, at least, wearing broad brim hats. Even within the settlement the clothing of the settlers was not suitable for the antipodean climate. According to Cedric Flower,[3]

'The convicts in coarse prison slops were probably better off than the marines in hot gaiters and red uniforms, the officials in great coats and powdered hair. Bush tore at breeches and stockinged legs; sandstone scuffed buckled shoes to pieces. The ragged state of everyone's clothes was soon a constant source of complaint.'

On 6 June 1789 Phillip again led an expedition to Broken Bay to further examine that harbour. Captain John Hunter, one of the party, records in his journal the party followed 'the sea coast to the north ward' encountering 'long sandy beaches to cross, which was a very fatiguing part of the journey.[4] On 7 June they examined Pittwater and spent the next four days investigating Broken Bay, returning to Pittwater on 14 June 1789.

Phillip led a large party of forty once more northwards on 29 June

Explorers at Broken Bay with native woman and child as painted by John Hunter

that year. During this expedition they travelled by boats up the river which Phillip named the Hawkesbury for the Earl of Liverpool, Baron Hawkesbury, then in charge of the colonies. On the fourteenth day of their journey, a wild squally day, they returned to Pittwater.

On 27 August 1789 Captain John Hunter led a party to Broken Bay to survey the area, including Pittwater. One of the party was Lieutenant Waterhouse, who during an earlier trip with Governor Phillip, had planted some crops. Waterhouse was delighted to discover during the survey journey 'the garden I made when we were last here; and found two pottatoes, two pumpkins, two melons, two rows of Indian corn, and two rows of french beans up, and looking exceeding well. I now sowed some Garlic.'[5] This was surely evidence of the fertility of the area.

The scholarly Lieutenant William Dawes, who established the first observatory on Point Maskelyne (later Dawes Point) at Sydney, walked along the northern beaches to Barrenjoey. Dawes mapped the coastline from Botany Bay to Broken Bay and the land as far west as the foothills of the Blue Mountains in 1791, the then known land of the colony.

With the establishment of the Government Farm at Parramatta by Phillip on 2 November 1788 and the township being laid out in 1790 interest in the northern peninsula waned. Its settlement and development was slow but is, nevertheless, an interesting part of the local history of Sydney.

Aborigines

For over 60,000 years the Aborigines have been resident on the Australian continent. The arrival of Europeans in 1788 at Botany Bay and subsequently at Port Jackson shattered their world.

The Aborigines who lived in the Broken Bay/Pittwater area were the Garigal. This group, or horde, belonged to a larger 'tribe', the Eora. N.B. Tindale[6] suggests five 'tribes' within the Sydney region. The Eora whose name meant 'the people' roamed the territory from Broken Bay to Botany Bay and inland to roughly Berowra Creek, Parramatta and Liverpool. The Eora would have included the

A 1789 view of Broken Bay by Lieutenant William Bradley of the First Fleet. In the foreground explorers and local Aborigines.

Guringai, Walumedegal, Wangal, Bidjigal, Cadigal and the powerful Gamaraigal, the latter remembered in the naming of the suburb of Cammeray. As Burnum Burnum notes, 'The precise number of clans and bands in the Sydney region, will never be known, but observations at the time of the fleet's arrival indicated that the Eora and Dharuk people were far more numerous than had been first estimated - probably around 3000 in the Sydney area, with half in the coastal regions from Botany Bay to Broken Bay.'[7] The Dharuk lived along the Hawkesbury River.

The officers of the First Fleet showed considerable interest in the Aborigines but as many of these officers had served in the American War of Independence they referred to the native inhabitants as 'Indians'. Their journals note encounters with the Aborigines recording details of weapons, fishing, shelters, appearance and behaviour. Dr. Worgan of the First Fleet claimed the women when near enough to accept a present were 'coy, shy, and timorous'[8]

During the first exploration of Broken Bay and Pittwater by the Governor together with his butler, some officers and a party of marines, it was noted 'the natives tho' very friendly appeared to be numerous.'[9] On 5 March 1788 the party was caught in a thunder squall and they met 'an Old Man and Boy' who showed them the best landing place and 'brought us a stick of Fire & some Water signifying to us that the rain was very cold, we gave them fish & the Governor exchanged some things for Spears...'[10]

The next day, when it was still raining, 'the Old man & boy followed us around to one of the Coves & shew'd us water. We stopped in a Cove on the E. side about 3 miles up, several women in Canoes were fishing two of them came ashore the one was Old & Ugly, the other a young Woman tall & was the handsomest woman I have seen amongst them, she was very big with Child...'[11] Bradley observed one woman making a fish hook 'from the inside of what is commonly called the pearl Oyster shell, by rubbing it down on the rocks until thin enough & then cut it circular with another, shape the hook with a sharp point rather bent in & not bearded or barbed'.[12] The women also gathered a kernel they fed to the children - 'they are a kind of nut growing in bunches somewhat like a pine top and are poisonous without being properly prepared.'[13]

In August 1788 Surgeon White noted in a bark 'hut' discovered at Broken Bay 'two very well made nets, some fishing lines not inferior to the nets, some spears, a stone hatchet of a very superior make to what they usually have, together with two vehicles for carrying water, one of cork, the other made out of the knot of a large tree hollowed. In this hut there were two pieces of coarse linen, which they must have obtained from some of our people, and everything about it bespoke more comfort and convenience than I have observed in any other.'[14] Reference is made during this trip of 'a path not very frequented'[15] presumably one of the many tracks used by the Aborigines around Sydney.

During Phillip's visit to Broken Bay in June 1789 Hunter records 'meeting a native woman concealing herself from our sight in the long grass. She had been employed in fishing, this miserable girl, who had just recovered from the smallpox, was very weak, and unable, from a swelling in one of her knees, to get off to any distance. She appeared to be about seventeen or eighteen years of age; she was very much frightened on our approaching her, and shed many tears, with piteous lamentations: we understood none of her expressions,[16] but felt much concern at the distress she seemed to suffer. We endeavoured all in our power to make her easy, and with the assistance of a few

expressions which had been collected from poor Arabanoo[17] while he was alive, we soothed her distress a little, and the sailors were immediately ordered to bring up some fire, which we placed before her: we pulled some grass, dried it by the fire, and spread around her to keep her warm; then we shot some birds, such as hawkes, crows, and gulls, skinned them, and laid them on the fire to broil together with some fish, which she eat. Next morning we visited her again, she had now got pretty much the better of her fears, and frequently called to her friends, who had left her, that the strangers were not enemies, but friends'.[18]

Within twelve months of the white arrival the Aborigines of the Sydney region were suffering the effects of that settlement. In 1789 an outbreak of what was believed to be smallpox ravaged the Aboriginal population.[19] As Captain Watkin Tench of the Marines noted 'An extraordinary calamity was now observed among the natives. Repeated accounts brought by our boats of finding bodies of the Indians in all the coves and the inlets of the harbour... (Port Jackson).'[20] From Hunter's account the smallpox had taken its toll at Broken Bay and Pittwater. Venereal disease had also been introduced among the Aborigines. It has been estimated that perhaps 3000 Aborigines lived around Sydney in 1788. Smallpox reduced this number by half.

Prior to white settlement and their eventual decimation in the Sydney region the Aborigines of Pittwater must have enjoyed a good lifestyle. There would have been adequate food, fish, water and shelter. The Aborigines of the Sydney area were a fishing people. Women fished with hook and line from canoes. Men used fishing spears called 'mooting'. When fish was scarce, which happened during winter, the Aborigines suffered. In the early days of settlement Phillip ordered that the fish caught for use in the settlement was to be shared with the Aborigines.

From the many shell middens discovered around the Sydney environs it is evident that shellfish and molluscs were an important dietary source. Seabirds and marine mammals also provided food. Phillip was speared at Manly when Bennelong and his companions were feasting on a whale washed ashore on a local beach.[21] There were kangaroos, wallabies and other marsupials and possum hunting was an important activity. Digging sticks were used by the women to obtain edible roots, and both witchetty grubs and eggs taken from hollow branches were another adjunct to the diet. There were the seeds of the burrawang palm, *(Macrozamia communis)*, parts of the giant gymea lily *(Doryanthus excelsa)*, the fruits of the lillypilly *(Acmena smithii)*, geebungs *(Persoonia spp.)* and the Port Jackson fig *(Ficus rubiginosa)*. As some of the native plants eaten by the white settlers made them ill the Aborigines obviously treated the plants to make them edible. The burrawang seeds were pounded and soaked for a week before being roasted in ashes. While rough shelters were constructed the Pittwater topography provided caves and rocky overhangs for shelter from the elements. That is not to say that life was at times not harsh. The officers observed the Aborigines sometimes shivering from the cold and the old man at Broken Bay signified the rain was very cold.

Their rock carvings, middens and cave stencils remain as mute reminders of these lost people. Jan Morris writes 'I sometimes feel myself haunted by a sense of loss, as though time is passing too fast, and frail black people are watching me out of the night somewhere, leaning on their spears'.[22]

Description and History of Pittwater

Entering Broken Bay, (which was named by Captain Cook on Monday, 7 May 1770 when he was off the coast and noted broken land 'which appeared to form a bay....')[23] the southern headland is Barrenjoey, rising some 110 metres from the sea. The area of Pittwater lies around this headland and is enclosed by West Head and Commodore Heights opposite Barrenjoey which forms the western boundary.

Pittwater, 16 nautical miles north of Port Jackson, is 8 kilometres long and 2 kilometres wide at its widest point. An arm or inlet of Broken Bay, the waters of Pittwater are deep and protected and within the national park area still bordered with heavily timbered hillsides.

Soundings of the waters of Pittwater were recorded during Governor Phillip's first visit in 1788. It was noted that the bar 'which runs across the entrance'[24] is '18 foot (5 1/2 metres) at low water' but within the bar the waters were '7 to 15 fathom feet'.[25] The shoal patch at Pittwater's entrance is locally called The Flats and stretches from West Head to Barrenjoey, up to Observation Head and across to the point between Great and Little Mackerel Beaches on the western shore. However there is plenty of water over The Flats for small craft. At the deepest point it is 2.7 metres. Beyond Observation Point the depth of Pittwater is about 5 fathoms.

In 1804 Governor Hunter, who had helped explore Pittwater in the early days of settlement, ordered a survey of the area. Even at that time the Aborigines were asking for land rights as the settlers were increasing around Pittwater and the Hawkesbury and they asked that portion of the foreshores be assigned to them. Hunter acceded to the request and land was assigned on

An aerial view of Barrenjoey and the northern peninsula in 1931.

the northside of the Hawkesbury. Following the 1804 survey Pittwater is placed 'in the Hundred of Packenham, in the County of Cumberland, and the Parish of Warrabeen'.

Surveyor William Romaine Govett (remembered by Govett's Leap, near Blackheath in the Blue Mountains) surveyed the coast from Port Jackson to Broken Bay in 1829. In his journal he describes Pittwater as 'a quiet inlet of the sea, protected from the boisterous waves without by a ridge of mountain, and a narrow sand-bar' forming 'a beautiful and romantic lake, and is found a convenient shelter in adverse weather'.[26] In the general area he noted the ridges were 'barren, rocky and precipitous',[27] that the peaks resembled 'the castellated ruins of a fortress',[28] that the Aborigines referred to the caves and rough rock shelters as 'gibbie gunyahs'[29] and he sighted a host of fly-

ing foxes. Govett had the foresight to see future development when the shores of Pittwater would 'give way to the ornamental villas of the rich and all these silent waters in times to come may resound with the festivities of the merry and the gay.'[30]

In 1838 nine years after Govett Captain Bethune made a naval survey of Broken Bay in HMS *Conway*. A further naval survey was made by Captain Stokes in HMS *Acharon* in 1851.

Captain F.W. Sidney surveyed the east coast of Australia, including Pittwater between 1868 and 1872. His chart shows a great variation of names: Scotland Island is Pitt Island; Careel Bay is Evening Bay; the southern entrance to Careel Bay is Stripe Bay; Lovett's Bay is Night Bay; Towlers Bay is Morning Bay.

Turning into Pittwater around Barrenjoey Headland past Shark Point one enters tranquil waters.

Barrenjoey Lighthouse

Barrenjoey is reputedly the Aboriginal name for a young kangaroo. Govett, in his journal states, 'A sand-bar connects that extraordinary headland with the main range.'[31]

Barrenjoey is majestic - a towering area of sandstone and bushland terminating the northern peninsula with the placid or wild waters of the Pacific Ocean and Broken Bay washing its foundations. The impressive stone lighthouse, 110 metres above the sea, is a beacon for mariners or landlubbers.

Even in 1855 there was a beacon here for mariners, a simple weatherboard building which only displayed a light during rough weather.

In 1863 it was proposed additional lighthouses would be erected on the Australian coast. One was planned for Barrenjoey and this proposal was vigorously supported by Robert Stewart, who was the member for East Sydney in the New South Wales Parliament. Two white towers, the Stewart Towers, were duly constructed and opened in 1868 for the grand sum of £385; £300 for the towers and £85 for two lanterns displaying white lights. The Stewart Towers were used for thirteen years.

The present lighthouse was designed by the eminent architect James Barnet (1827-1904), creator of many of Sydney's Victorian buildings, including the General Post Office. This lighthouse was rather more expensive - £16,695. The foundation stone was laid on 15 April 1880 by the architect's daughter, Rosa. To reach Barrenjoey the party of 'notabilities', including Mrs. Barnet, the architect's wife, who attended the ceremony endured a long and somewhat fatiguing journey. They left Circular Quay at a quarter past seven in the morning in the steamer *Emu* bound for Manly Beach, from where they were to go overland in vehicles. The morning was stormy and the harbour was overspread with fog. During the trip the fog cleared and they were met at the wharf by three vehicles and transported to Cohen's Hotel for breakfast. The *Sydney Morning Herald* report noted that the scenery after leaving Manly, 'Sydney's favourite marine suburb, was dull and uninteresting; but as we went on the features of the landscape changed, and the level tracts covered with stunted timber and brushwood gave place to undulating country, with trees of large dimensions, though evidently not of much commercial value.'[32] The beautiful ferns were also noted. There was an exciting crossing of Narrabeen Lagoon with the men in the party offering their services as 'life-boys',[33] to which the ladies responded with peals of laughter. On arrival at Pittwater the writer stated 'For miles it stretched towards the entrance to the mouth of the Hawkesbury; while, on either side, bold headlands, crowned to their summits with timber, and looking like great sentinels, rose from the water's edge. Expressions of wonder at the beauty of the scene were heard on all sides, and the fact that this lovely place is so little known to denizens of the metropolis was freely commented on.'[34] At Bayview the party boarded the steamer, *Florrie* to transport them to Barrenjoey. The *Florrie* was owned by Mr. Jeanneret who was among the party. From the steamer a whale boat carried the visitors to the jetty where Mr. Banks, the contractor of the lighthouse, had a '"tram-car", or rather trolley, in waiting'[35] to carry the ladies to the top of Barrenjoey. The tramcar was drawn by two horses and had a brake 'so powerful that the car can be stopped almost in its own length when going down the steepest incline'.[36] The tramway had been constructed 1000 feet (304 metres) to the lighthouse to carry the

kerosene for the light, the timber for the railway being drawn up by two horses. The *Sydney Morning Herald* wrote that Miss Barnet was presented with a solid silver trowel with an ivory handle to lay the foundation stone and a mallet of tulip wood was used for the ceremony. Bottles containing the scroll, papers, coins and a medallion of Queen Victoria were placed under the stone. One of the party, Mr. Greville, made a rather fulsome speech

'With a few light touches of this pretty piece of metal and a few taps of the mallet you will lay the first stone of a tower which will be the guide and safeguard of many future voyages. Above the spot on which you stand there will rise a noble beacon - the silent sentinel of the storm-tossed mariner, the shining monitor, warning those who brave the perils of the deep to shun the more obdurate dangers of these callous rocks'.[37]

During the construction work two of the workmen died.

Frederick William Stark, a blacksmith, was killed and George Cobb drowned. Both were buried beside St John's Church at Pittwater.

The Barrenjoey Lighthouse was first lit on 1 August 1881 by the lighthouse keeper, George Mulhall. Local legend says four years later the old lighthouse keeper, aged 71 years, was struck and killed by lightning. It was claimed his body was burnt almost to a cinder. However Jervis Sparks in his Tales From Barranjoey refutes this colourful tale stating Mulhall's death certificate reveals he died of apoplexy (a stroke) after three days of illness. Mulhall's remains were buried in a small walled enclosure close to the light. Beside him is his wife, Mary, who died on 28 December 1886. Mulhall's epitaph reads

All ye that come my grave to see
Prepare in time to follow me.
Repent at once without delay,
For I in haste was called away.

Barrenjoey Lighthouse is sited at latitude 33° 35' south; longitude

Henry Boulton and a sled of coal bound for Barrenjoey Lighthouse.

Barrenjoey Lighthouse and buildings in 1890.

151° 20' east. The lighthouse gives four flashes every twenty seconds visible from seaward for forty kilometres at an elevation of 113 metres. Bushwalkers face an energetic toil from the beach to the headland's summit where they can gaze at Mulhall's grave and enjoy the breathtaking views. The summit is named Gledhill Lookout for the founder and for many years President of the Manly Warringah & Pittwater Historical Society. In a time when others cared little for our origins Percy Gledhill was an indefatigable worker in the field of local history.

Since 1968 Jervis Sparks and his wife Bridget have lived at a cottage at Barrenjoey Lighthouse. He has founded the Barranjoey (sic) Historical Resources Centre, researched the lighthouse and headland history and likes to keep people informed about the area.

On 22 June 1992 Sparks organised a ceremony for the unveiling of a plaque to the first lighthouse keeper, George Mulhall. Twenty of Mulhall's descendants were contacted and came to honour their ancestor at the ceremony. The plaque reads,

George Mulhall was the first official light keeper on Barranjoey Headland. Firstly at the Stewart Towers, from 1868 to 1881, then at the Barranjoey Lighthouse.
He was born in the colony and died

of natural causes.
His son George followed on as
headkeeper until his
retirement in 1891.

Sparks prefers an earlier spelling of 'Barranjoey'. The present use of Barrenjoey was standardized in 1976 by the Geographical Names Board.

On 8 September 1992 it was announced that Barrenjoey Lighthouse was one of eight lighthouses which are to become redundant.

Because of better navigational technology the major shipping companies, which fund lighthouses through levies, claim they are no longer needed.

The Boat Owners Association of New South Wales suggested the introduction of a fee on a user-pays principle in addition to annual boating licences and other interested parties are hopeful of stopping the discontinuation of the light on Barrenjoey.

Barrenjoey Customs House

For many years the whole area in this vicinity was Barranjoey and it has been spelt Barrenjuee, Barranjo, Barenja and Barrenjee. In such a remote area smuggling was rife, shades of the old days of,

Watch the wall my darling,
While the gentlemen ride by.[38]

One story relates that the famous Billy Blue, the Jamaican convict who was transported for stealing a bag of sugar and for whom Sydney's Blue's Point is named, arranged for contraband rum to be offloaded at Pittwater. He then had it transported overland to the north side of Sydney Harbour. To eradicate this type of heinous crime the Collector of Customs had asked for a customs officer to be stationed at Broken Bay. On 6 August 1841 M.J. Gibbes, the Collector of Customs, issued a notice in which he pointed out that any 'person giving information is entitled to a reward without his name being divulged of one third of what sum may accrue to the seizing officer from the sale of such goods, however large it may be.'[39]

One opportunist seized his chance when the *Fair Barbarian* sailed from Sydney in 1842 bound for Lombok (Indonesia) but in fact slipped into Broken Bay, unloaded a cargo of spirits and departed for Hobart. Two hundred casks of brandy and a quantity of inferior Mauritius rum were off-loaded and hidden near Cowan Creek. Charles Swancott writes of the events in The Brisbane Water Story.[40] Two settlers, Robert Henderson and John Farrell were charged at the Water Police Court, Sydney, on 25 August 1842, with the concealment of spirits at Cowan Creek.

An informer, John Tumey, said he was cutting timber at Cowan Creek in mid June when he found 200 small casks of brandy and 29 casks of rum. The casks were under a rock and all were marked with white letters. Tumey, however, could not read or write and was unable to say what the letters were. He said he rode a horse from Pittwater to Middle Harbour and swam to Sydney to inform the authorities. He returned with the Superintendent of Water Police, Captain Browne in the Police schooner *Ariel* to Broken Bay. With an Inspector of Police, Captain Browne and a crew of eight they then travelled in a whaleboat up the Hawkesbury River. During the journey they encountered a boat which contained three men including Robert Henderson, a pannikin of brandy and a paint brush wet with black paint.

A mile further on in Cowan

Creek the casks of rum and brandy
were found. The identifying marks
on the rum casks were obliterated
with black paint and the brandy
casks holystoned and the original
white paint marks rubbed off. One
cask had been overlooked and bore
the mark *D. & Co.'Triton'*.

Henderson's solicitor had the
case dismissed on a legal technicali-
ty and a fresh information was filed
for aiding and abetting the con-
veyance of the spirits. Again the
solicitor had the case dismissed
pleading since his client had been
acquitted of concealing the liquor,
the Bench could not entertain a
fresh information for its con-
veyance; the Customs could not
prosecute a person for both convey-
ing, concealing or aiding and abetting so that £100 damages could be
obtained for each offence. The
Bench agreed the plea was a good
one.

In November the same year the
Sydney merchants of the cargo
Robert Glasgow Dunlop and John
Ross with their sureties appeared
before the Supreme Court for non-
fulfilment of their bonds. Instead of
being shipped to Lombok the goods
had been smuggled ashore at
Broken Bay. Dunlop was fined
£5000 and Ross £6000.

In 1843 a Customs House was
established below the Barrenjoey
Headland. Earlier, c.1804 south of
this area and below Observation
Point an elderly man named Pat
Flynn had a well cultivated garden.
He sold his vegetables at a cheap
price and told tales of a wild storm
when the ocean swept right across
the isthmus. Fishermen were active
on Pittwater as early as 1807 and
the NSW Calendar and General
Post Office Directory of 1832
records '3 Old Fisherman'. The
1828 Census records one Edward
Flinn, aged seventy four years, as a
fisherman at 'Pitt Water'. Flinn had
arrived as a convict on the
Friendship with the First Fleet in
1788 sentenced to seven years transportation. The Customs House was
manned by the customs officer, a
coxswain and five crew for the customs boat. In 1846 the
Commissioners of Customs in
London claimed in 1846 the station
had 'checked' the smuggling at
Broken Bay and that it should be a
permanent establishment. It seems
more likely that the ingenuity of the
local smugglers sometimes bested
the authorities despite an 8 foot
(186 cm) tall soldier which stood
near a cave close to the lighthouse.
Resplendent in painted white

The Customs House, Palm Beach 1908.

trousers, scarlet coat, helmet and armed with tin sword and scabbard this valiant officer threatened all those bound on smuggling until white ants ate his wooden legs and he tumbled to the earth. Maybanke Anderson[41] comments, 'So passes the glory of the world'. However the *Sydney Morning Herald* of 6 April 1861 mentions 'Several soldiers, made out of trees, as large as life, and painted, are placed about, and might actually serve as landmarks to vessels entering these complicated waters.'

Illicit stills flourished in remote areas and customs officials were to monitor the illegal distillation. The customs officer had many duties, inspecting vessels moored from Brisbane Water to Dangar Island and the Pittwater inlets and inspecting and maintaining channel markers and buoys as well as the general surveillance work.

The Customs House was sited on land owned by the Wentworth family which had become part of the Darley estate after Katherine Wentworth's marriage to Captain Darley (see page 25). In 1881 the land was finally transferred to the State of New South Wales and Darley compensated for £1,250. The Darleys had earlier been paid £50 per annum for rent of the land.

In 1862 new buildings were erected at the Customs Station and an overhanging cliff rock blasted with gun powder. The customs officer, then termed a 'Coast Waiter' feared it might fall on his house and sent his wife 'to a place of safety.'[42]

The Customs House survived until fire destroyed the building in 1976. In March 1981 the National Trust of Australia (NSW) prepared a paper on the Customs House site. It stated the site of the Customs House was clearly identifiable by floor surfaces, chimney bases and contours. The site of the customs jetty, although demolished, was also identifiable and there was a narrow track with traces of irregular cobbled paving winding eastwards.

Barrenjoey

In 1872 the first school at Barrenjoey was located in a former boatman's cottage, south of the Customs Station. The children of the local settlers and farmers were transported by boat or walked to the schoolhouse. On bright sunny days it was a pleasant approach to school but on wild wet winter days the attendance must have dropped dramatically. Jervis Sparks gives an interesting account of the schools of Barrenjoey in 'Tales from Barranjoey'.

A telegraph was opened to 'Barrenjuey' in 1869 and a Post Office in 1871. In 1876 it took two days for telegrams to be sent from Manly to the peninsula. The *Maitland,* a passenger carrying paddle-wheel steamship, was wrecked during a heavy gale near Cape Three Points between Sydney and Newcastle on 5 May 1898.

The vessel had cleared Sydney Heads and initially made good progress but there was a howling gale. The ship was taking too much water and Captain Skinner decided to turn round and try to shelter in Broken Bay. The deck cargo was thrown overboard but when one of the boats was launched it was smashed to pieces.

At a quarter to six in the morning the *Maitland* crashed on rocks and broke in halves. The captain asked for volunteers to get a line ashore. A saloon passenger and two seamen tried to get the line ashore, all failed but managed to survive the wild seas. Another passenger John Russell with two of the crew then made an attempt. The two crew members drowned but Russell secured the line to a boulder and the remaining passengers and crew struggled ashore through the heavy breakers. However fifteen of the passengers and eleven crew perished. The storm became known as the Maitland gale. The keepers at Barrenjoey had contacted the Coast Waiter and reported the tragedy to Sydney. Below the grandeur of Barrenjoey Headland the peninsula narrows back towards Palm Beach. Within Pittwater there is the long curve of Station or Barrenjoey Beach. On quiet weekdays a few aluminium boats rest on the sand and a shag splashes in the water. There are a few remaining shells on the beach and the scene is dramatic and romantic with the distant backdrop of bushclad hills and a few white triangular sails of the yachts gliding across Pittwater. During weekends small children paddle at the water's edge, sunbathers rest on the sand, and wind surfers skim across the waters like gaudy butterflies.

In earlier times further south on land near Palm Beach Jetty Ah Chuey managed a fish-drying plant. In the 1870s this prosperous business purchased fish from local fishermen at five shillings a dozen for schnapper. The fish were dried and salted in brine at the plant. The refuse from the works was used as fertiliser for the vegetable gardens the Chinese tended in the area. The salted fish were shipped to Chinese outlets in Sydney, Melbourne and to China. At the time there were great quantities of mutton shell fish or Venus' Ear (Heliotis Tuberculata) clinging to the rocks. The Chinese considered the flesh a great delicacy and old-timers spoke of mounds of discarded shells close to the Chinese gardens. Overseas the shells, exported from California where the species was also plentiful, were used in the manufacture of buttons and for pearl inlaying.

The narrow isthmus of land at Palm Beach was, until comparatively recent times, a favourite reserve for campers and caravaners, many of them permanent dwellers. It was the only area in the peninsula where camping was permitted and fees were to be paid in advance - £2/2/- per week or ten shillings per day. The camping area was closed by Warringah Shire Council in the 1960s. Now named Governor Phillip Park the peninsula is shared with Palm Beach Golf Course. Their club house is across Beach Road.

Golfing fashions c.1920s on the land between Sunrise Road and Barrenjoey. The Palm Beach golf course was not at the time properly laid out.

Palm Beach Golf Club

It was in the jazz era of the early 1920s that the Palm Beach Golf Club was established. It was founded officially in 1924 under the Presidency of C.R. Crossman who was supported by the foundation members C. Broughton, S.H. Hammond, G.H. Hitchcock, S.B. Hooper, B.L. Houghton and E.R. Moser. The original clubhouse was a small cottage owned by the Hammond family on a site adjoining the present building. S.H. Hammond was the father of the singer Joan Hammond and she learned to play golf at Palm Beach. She was one of golf's great players in the 1930s.

The present clubhouse was opened on 15 October 1965 on the site of Dormy, a small cottage which had its interior walls removed. It had been rented from A. Oxlade for 30 shillings a week from 1 February 1933 before the Golf Club purchased the property some years later.

When the golf links was first established it is said the greens had to be enclosed with wire fencing to prevent grazing cattle from venturing on them. The links were leased from Warringah Shire Council on the proviso that the Golf Club would collect the camping fees from the council camping area in Governor Phillip Park. The campers, themselves, enjoyed the golf links and during the Christmas holiday period there was often a field of 200 golfers per day playing golf. The golf course is still leased through the local council who hold it in trust for the Department of Lands. It is open to the public on Mondays, Wednesdays and Fridays and at weekends outside Members'

competitions. The Pro Shop and course facilities are wholly managed and maintained by Palm Beach Golf Club through its Directors, Secretary-Manager and its membership.

The Club House enjoys views of both Pittwater and the Barrenjoey Headland and on the greens opposite in earlier years both Australian Prime Minister W.M. 'Billy' Hughes and Sir Dallas Brooks, Governor of Victoria, often enjoyed a game of golf. The course is only 4100 metres long but very tight. Par is 64 and one has to be very accurate with iron shots. The nine hole course covers nearly 10 hectares.

Few golf courses have a more magnificent location than Palm Beach Golf Club. One interesting photograph in the Club House is of a severe hail storm which occurred on 28 August 1956; it shows the golf course carpeted with the hailstones so that it resembles a snowy scene at Palm Beach!

Aquatic Airways/Sydney Harbour Seaplanes

From the golf course a seaplane may be viewed rising from the waters of Pittwater. Aquatic Airways, Australia's Coastal Airline, began operations in December, 1975 operating a Cessna 185 floatplane, VH-FGC, from Palm Beach to Sydney. It carried three passengers. In 1977 a second Cessna 206, VH-FVW, was purchased to carry five passengers. At the time tourists were wishing to view Sydney from the air and to cater for the demand additional flights from Gosford on the Central Coast and Rose Bay on Sydney Harbour commenced. The 'planes were also used as a commuter service by business people flying the Gosford, Palm Beach and Rose Bay route. The service proved so popular that an additional Cessna was purchased in 1979 from Sweden.

In September 1980 the company was granted a Regular Public Transport licence by the Department of Aviation to run an airline service from Port Stephens to Palm Beach, and later to Rose Bay. This enabled Aquatic Airways to apply to I.A.T.A. for a world airline accreditation which was subsequently granted, the international designator being VZ.

A 1920s view of the area occupied by Palm Beach Golf Club. Note Lion Island.

With the growth of the company two of the early Cessnas were sold and a De Havilland Beaver from the United States of America purchased. This 'plane was capable of carrying eight passengers and the windows were modified to give better views. In 1982 Aquatic Airways was awarded the ATIA Enterprise Award for Tourism in New South Wales.

The company had four Australian-made Nomads and three Beavers. On 21 January, 1991 the North Shore area of Sydney was struck by a devastating storm. This subsequently swept across Pittwater damaging one of Aquatic Airways' floating Beavers, later rebuilt, and the company office.

The seaplanes were a familiar sight taking off and landing from Rose Bay on Sydney Harbour and at Pittwater and the company offered a number of scenic and charter flights enabling passengers to view the full beauty of these areas. Aquatic Airways ceased operations in 1993. The company has been replaced with Sydney Harbour Seaplanes flying regular services over Pittwater to Newcastle and back, as well as charter and sightseeing flights. The company will also operate to Gosford and Port Stephens and may also operate to the South Coast. Sydney Harbour Seaplanes will continue the work pioneered by Aquatic Airways and in 1994 plan to refurbish their fleet of planes.

Atlantis Divers

Close by the office of the seaplanes is Atlantis Divers where enthusiasts may enjoy this activity. Atlantis Divers have been located here for fourteen years and offer charter boat dives off Barrenjoey Headland and nearside coastline. Diving attracts both local, interstate and overseas visitors providing good diving in unpolluted waters. The diving boats carry eight people a trip and operate four times a day.

One dive close to Barrenjoey Headland is at the Dragons. The weedy sea dragons live in the kelp in 14 metres of water and are in the locality all year, so they may be viewed on every dive. Off the headland is the Sponge Gardens covering approximately 18 metres. Here divers may see large schooling kingfish, numerous varieties of sponges and gorgonia. Atlantis Divers offer various courses including basic scuba courses.

One of the company's dives is on the wreck of a harbour tug, the *Valient*. It sank in May 1981 and lies 26 metres deep, 400 metres off the ocean side of Barrenjoey. Mike Buesnel has dived on Valient some 300 times and actually saw the vessel sink on a foul squally day when a two metre to three metre swell was rolling around Barrenjoey. *Valient* was being towed by a barge when it lost the tow and the tug sank in a few minutes. Buesnel located the wreck seven days later 'with a big shoal of Kingfish encircling her mast'.[43] Mike has observed the changes to the tug. He says there are growths of white soft coral, the moray eels inhabit it at night, 'a big blue groper'[44] keeps watch on the bridge during the evening, there are red banded shrimps, cuttle fish, blue swimmer crabs, kingfish, yellowtail, trevally, a pair of large John Dory and the odd hammerhead (shark) wanders past. 'But that was always *yesterday*',[45] Mike claims.

The *Valient* was commissioned in 1945 by the Ministry of Munitions, a wartime department. Overall length is 23 metres, beam 5.5 metres. The vessel was last used as a fire boat by the Port of Melbourne Authority.

The company also carries out

wharf repairs and maintenance on the many jetties and wharves around Pittwater, underwater construction, salvage and recovery and precision dredging.

A small coffee shop near the airways and diving offices provides refreshments and the tables overlook the sweep of Pittwater. A young American couple, now resident in the area, sit in the sun enjoying coffee and lunch and think they have found paradise. Few would disagree.

Palm Beach

Barrenjoey Headland, Palm Beach and most of the Whale Beach area was a grant of 400 acres (160 hectares) to Naval Surgeon John Napper on 16 March 1816 by Governor Macquarie. Napper named the estate Larkfield. It was later owned by Robert Campbell, a nephew of the famous Robert Campbell of Campbell's Wharf in Sydney, then Dr. D'Arcy Wentworth, father of William Charles Wentworth. Dr. Wentworth bequeathed the land to his daughter, Katherine.

On the coastal side of the peninsula the yellow beach sands stretch from the Palm Beach rock baths to end under the shadow of Barrenjoey Headland. Palm Beach was named for the indigenous cabbage tree palms which provided the colony's early settlers with the palm fronds to make cabbage tree hats, a popular colonial headwear.

In 1900 land was subdivided but blocks of 74 acres (30 hectares) failed to sell. By 1912 Sunrise Cottage at the start of Sunrise Hill was one of the few residences. This is where Albert Verrills lived. He built many of the early houses at Palm Beach and around 1915 built a new residence for his family in Barrenjoey Road behind Barrenjoey House. Another early residence was the Cabbage Tree Club, built as a home in 1913 by W. Chorley who was a military and civilian tailor in Sydney. This house is integrated in the Palm Beach Surf Life Saving Club with a large two storey home with arched concrete foundations built in 1917 by T. Peters, a con-

struction engineer. The Curlewis family built Willeroon. Clive Pemberton Curlewis was an early President of the local surf club and uncle of Judge Adrian Curlewis who was President of the Surf Life Saving organisation for many years. The Horderns of the earlier city

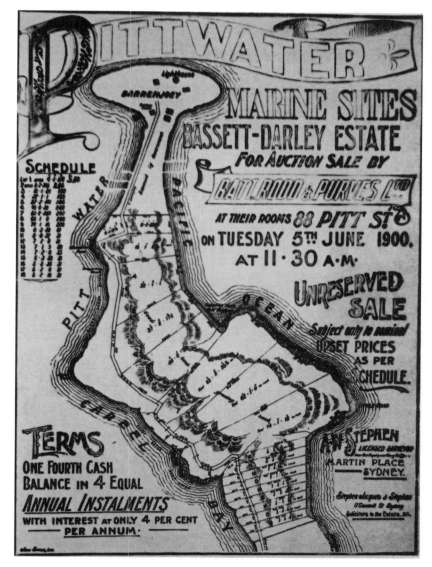

An auction notice of 1900 of the Bassett-Darley Estate, Palm Beach.

Barrenjoey House in 1917. Behind is the home of the Verrills family.

An Easter visit to the beach in 1929 by the Seaman family.

occurred and increased numbers of commuters lived on the peninsula.

Palm Beach became fashionable and many North Shore residents made holiday bookings to meet country friends and enjoy a relaxing holiday together. The hills overlooking Palm Beach were called locally Spin Hill, an abbreviation for Spinster's Hill, as it was said many maiden ladies lived there, and Pill Hill because of the proliferation of homes owned by Macquarie Street doctors.

There are some interesting sandstone houses at Palm Beach, several built by Lawrie Gallagher. Florida House in Florida Road has thick stone walls built from stone quarried on the site. Gallagher built his own home next to Florida House. His interests were many. A member of the Manly Warringah and Pittwater Historical Society Lawrie Gallagher once led an excursion to Scotland Island to point out carvings which he believed were made by Spanish sailors long before the arrival in Australia of Captain Cook or Governor Phillip. He had

store built Kalva in the 1920s and R.J. Hordern was responsible for the planting of the Norfolk Island pines along the beachfront in 1914-1915. Hordern Park was part of the family estate.

By the 1920s Palm Beach was more accessible. Because of its earlier inaccessibility it had escaped over-development. Only the affluent could afford to build here, often a second home. The greatest changes occurred after World War II when more development

a keen interest in metaphysical subjects and an inherent Irish charm.

High on the hillside overlooking the beach and with expansive views to Barrenjoey and Broken Bay the late Gerald H. Robinson created a Bible Garden. Begun in 1962 Robinson was inspired after a visit to a similar garden at Bangor in Wales. He filled the garden with plants mentioned in the Bible and Middle East wildflowers such as cyclamen, lupins, irises, hyacinths, statice, crocuses and tulips. He established a Display Room with Christian literature and other items such as pressed flowers from the Holy Land. Robinson desired the garden in Mitchell Road to continue after his death and bequeathed the land to a Trust. Sadly the garden is neglected but the views are splendid.

The 190 'bendy' bus runs from Wynyard to Palm Beach, Sydney's longest bus route, a journey accomplished in approximately one and a quarter hours. It follows the main road and northern beaches and there are glimpses of Pittwater as it nears its destination. During summer months the beach is popular and brightly coloured beach umbrellas dot the sand; a typical Sydney scene.

Duke Paoa Kahanamoku introduced the skill of standing on surf boards to Sydney beaches in 1915. Here members of the Palm Beach Surf Life Saving Club (founded 1921) pose with the old style massive boards.

All hands needed! Mrs Seaman of Palm Beach helping to dig out a bogged car on a peninsula dirt road uphill from Maitlands c. 1920s/1930s.

A festive occasion at Gonsalves Boatshed at Palm Beach in 1949.

Photographer Johnson and models at Palm Beach in the 1940s.

Looking down on Gonsalves Boatshed in earlier years. West Head on left.

South Palm Beach with the bathing shed on right. Note bushclad hillside. 1920-1925.

Going fishing. A c.1930s scene in Pacific Road, Palm Beach.

A family day at Palm Beach c.1930s. Note cars on roadway.

Motoring in a Fiat in 1909 from Palm Beach (Pittwater side) over Observation Hill to Barrenjoey. The ladies are wearing motoring veils.

Where are they now? The Surf Board Club on Palm Beach c.1960.

The second Palm Beach clubhouse, situated in Hordern Park, provided more accommodation.

The first clubhouse of the Palm Beach Surf Life Saving Club.

Mrs Bell sews on a quiet veranda at Palm Beach c.1920.

Gow's Wharf at Pittwater, Palm Beach in 1918. The road winding away in the distance leads only as far as the area now occupied by Palm Beach Golf Club.

*The Palm Beach boatshed
long before the area was
developed.*

East Pittwater – Snapperman Beach

On Pittwater from Observation Point to Sand Point stretches Snapperman Beach. Around 1912 Gow's boatshed was located south of Observation Point. There was also a small wharf and a ferry meandered around Pittwater from Newport to various destinations on the estuary. Transport was difficult, if not non-existent in some areas and access to Palm Beach was principally by launch from Church Point.

Things have not changed all that much. There is a small park and a public wharf with a ferry service operating to The Basin and Mackerel Beach. Weekenders and holiday makers crowd the ferry for a scenic round trip to Coasters Retreat, Bonnie Doon, The Basin, Currawong and Mackerel Beach. There is a Palm Beach/Patonga service and a sixty kilometre scenic Hawkesbury River Cruise covering Pittwater, Broken Bay, Patonga, Cowan, the Hawkesbury River and Cowan Waters. The sparkling waters, blue skies and distant bushland areas give Pittwater a perpetual holiday atmosphere.

At Gonsalves Boatshed - 'Boatbuilders, Repairs, Slipping, Mooring, Hire Boats' - several yachts are on the slips and the hulls are being scraped and cleaned. A more superb workplace would be difficult to locate. The name of the boatshed comes from a local family. The Gonsalves family are believed to have originated in the Azores, the volcanic islands in the North Atlantic Ocean reputedly discovered by Diogo de Senill (or Sevilha), a pilot of the King of Portugal about 1427. Local Pittwater resident Carl Gonsalves believes his great grandparents came to Australia in the 1850s. One son was connected with the law courts in Sydney while another went to sea. His grandparents were fishing people at Rose Bay on Sydney Harbour and fished up the coast to Broken Bay. They used to offload their catch at Brooklyn as there was ice available there, return to Pittwater and stay overnight at Portuguese Beach. There is perhaps some credence in the claim that the origin of the name of the beach stems from their camp in the area. They would return to Rose Bay the next day, again fishing the coastal waters. The family spent holidays at Pittwater and eventually in 1917 decided to settle in the area.

An interesting local publication is the free monthly independent paper *Pittwater Life*. In Volume 2, No. 1, an article on Peter Kershaw, now the 'driving force' at Gonsalves Boatshed, talks about his restoration of the yacht Utiekah II. Kershaw found the yacht at Lovett Bay and decided to restore. Utiekah II dates from 1911 and was built in Melbourne for a teacher of Geelong Grammar 'Spud' O'Giles. He used the yacht to take students and other young men on sailing trips around Tasmania. Later Utiekah II was owned by Harold Nossiter, Australia's first round the world sailor. The yacht is a 42 footer (12.8 metres) and had a 68 foot (20 metre) timber mast. In her day she

A view above Gonsalves Boatshed at Palm Beach showing Snapperman Beach and Pittwater.

Peter Kershaw and mate of Gonsalves Boatshed, Palm Beach.

was the fastest yacht on Sydney Harbour. Peter Kershaw says the yacht was also once owned by Dorothea McKellar but is unsure when Utiekah II arrived on Pittwater.[46] Peter's wife, Li (Lisa), says they have had the yacht for seven or eight years and it was while restoring the deck that a plaque was discovered listing the various races Utiekah II had won. When that plaque was removed another was found beneath it bearing Dorothea Mackellar's name. The restoration is a labour of love and hopefully one day Utiekah II will once more sail the waters of Pittwater.

Across the main road from the boatshed and park are the local shops and picnickers wander back and forth for ice creams and drinks. High on the hillside the houses set amid thick bush and foliage enjoy the views across Pittwater.

Sand Point to Careel Bay

On the run from Palm Beach to Careel Bay among the houses there is heavily timbered country and access at several points to the shores of Pittwater. Across the expanse of Pittwater the view is to the sweep of forested hills with small beaches at the distant water's edge. The white sails of yachts and the local crowded ferry heading for a distant wharf are the only signs of activity. West Head is a theatrical backdrop and in Broken Bay is the looming presence of Lion Island and the promontories of the land across the bay. Red plastic streamers flutter in the breeze from a moored motor boat to repel seagulls who choose instead to walk nonchalantly along the small beach.

How remote it must have felt in the early days! Following his walk from Manly to Pittwater in 1792 Lieutenant William Dawes subsequently published a map. The high land above Careel Bay is marked 'good pasture for sheep.'

Pittwater is viewed now as a desirable residential area but the earlier settlers must have found life hard. The early farms would have been surveyed by James Meehan (1774-1826) who was transported following the Irish rising of 1798. He was assigned to Acting Surveyor-General Charles Grimes from 1803 to 1820. Nearly all the land surveys in the colony in this period were carried out by James Meehan.

The Pittwater area was fertile for Maybanke Anderson[47] records that excellent crops of oats were grown on the flats at Mona Vale, later Brock's Flat. Another pioneer Mrs. Boulton liked to tell of her adventures when she carried her butter and eggs by dray to Manly. Anderson further claims 'John Collins grew good wheat on his farm at Careel Bay, and took it in his boat to one of Singleton's mills on the river.'[48] A memorial sent by the Singleton brothers to Governor Macquarie in 1820 located their two water mills on Crown lands, 'the one at Kurry Jong, and the other opposite to the Lower Branch of the Hawkesbury River.'[49]

Shipbuilding was an early industry on Pittwater and tranquil inlets resounded to the sound of saw and hammer. One of the earliest vessels was the *Geordy* built by emancipist convict Andrew Thompson (see Scotland Island). Firewood was carried by vessels from Broken Bay to Sydney.

Because of the lack of lime for mortar in the colony shells were crushed and burnt to obtain the lime. The shell gatherers ventured as far as Pittwater and the men engaged in this occupation lived in huts around the area. The shells were carried by vessel to Sydney from Brisbane Water and Pittwater to Kennedy's Limeburners Wharf near Jones's Wharf at Millers Point, Sydney. The name of Lime Street (no longer in existence) at Millers Point came from a group of limeburners who were located further south in Darling Harbour from the 1830s and 1840s.

Careel Bay at the turn of the century when it was a long way from Sydney town.

Careel Bay when cows grazed there.

Careel Bay

The charm of Pittwater lies in its bays and inlets. Careel Bay (earlier Evening Bay) lies between Stokes Point and the peninsula where it narrows at Whale Beach on the ocean. The eastern side of Careel Bay is bordered by Hitchcock Park. Originally there was a swamp at the headwaters of Careel Bay and tidal flats and mangroves were reclaimed as land at a time when the importance of mangrove swamps was not appreciated. Hitchcock Park has sporting facilities, the Careel Bay Ovals and the Avalon Soccer Club. There is a 'Dog Exercise Area'. Etival Road borders the park and feathery casuarinas and a tangle of blue morning glory creeper lead to the mudflats and shoreline reserve area. Across the wet mud march battalions of tiny crabs. Upturned boats and canoes lie idly on a grassy bank near a clump of banana palms and coral trees loved by the rainbow lorikeets. The waters of Pittwater are reflective and the mood is peaceful and lazy.

Stokes Point recalls a convict who ended his days as a boatbuilder on Pittwater. Maybank Anderson[50] depicts him as a colourful character wrongfully arrested for stealing a handkerchief who, at Pittwater on Sundays, dressed as a dandy of the Beau Brummell era complete with bottle green coat, a stock at his neck and tall hat. In London Stokes had been a ladies' shoemaker and in the rough lifestyle of Pittwater was noted for his courteous manner.

Stokes Point was sometimes referred to as Stripe Point, in fact some locals still use the name.

There were several boatbuilders at Careel Bay. Charles Swancott[51] claims the first boats were built by a man named Bradbury. Stokes and another, Williams, had their slips south of Stokes Point and in 1855 George Green launched the *Architect* at the bay. His son, Dick, became a champion sculler.

Careel Boat Services on the shores of Careel Bay link the present with the past as boats are hauled up to their slip. The boatshed has had various owners and was earlier Fred's Boatshed run by Fred Shearer but for some 25 years it has been owned by the Royal Sydney Yacht Squadron. The boatshed provides moorings and boat repairs.

Mud flats and mangrove swamps still survive at Careel Bay. Rowing boats sit on the tidal flats and two women, their children and a dog wander across the mud like a scene from an early Australian impressionist painting. The modern homes here have gardens of native and exotic trees, bright purple tibouchina and pale blue plumbago and there are the soft sounds of bird calls.

Much of the land around Careel Bay was a grant to Father Therry (1790-1864). Therry, the first official Catholic priest in the colony, arrived in Sydney on 3 May 1820. He was later favoured by Governor Bourke who granted the priest 1200 acres (486 hectares) at Pittwater in 1833 and 280 acres (113 hectares) in 1837. Therry named portion of his land Mt. Patrick. Portion of the land at Careel Bay was called the Township of Brighton or Josephtown. There are streets named Patrick, Joseph and Therry at Careel Bay. An energetic man Father Therry sank coal shafts near Bilgola Head. He was accused by Archbishop Polding of having wasted £12,000 on this and other schemes.

Therry's land at Careel Bay must have been fertile for Maybanke Anderson[52] claims in the 1870s the Mulhall brothers sailed from Rushcutters Bay in Sydney Harbour to collect sacks of grass at the bay for stock feed.

Therry himself became merely a parish priest after the arrival of Bishop Polding in 1835. He had worked hard in the early years to lay the foundations of Catholicism in Australia and died at Balmain on 25 May 1864. Father Therry is buried in the crypt of St Mary's Cathedral in Sydney, the church he founded.

Avalon

The land from Careel Bay back to Avalon is an area of modern suburban streets with foreshore roads giving views over Pittwater to its olive green hills. In 1833 one Thomas Warner was granted 50 acres (20 hectares) here.

Avalon has a famous curving surfing beach where once huge sandhills stretched back to what is now the recreation reserve. The busy shopping area offers a variety of interesting shops and there is a holiday mood. At a pavement tearoom the scarlet, green and blue rainbow lorikeets feed in the native shrubs and sometimes come to the table to share a sugar bowl. Saturday shoppers enjoy coffee, overseas newspapers and an excellent selection of books, videos and compact discs at Bookoccino.

One may wonder at the name Avalon, the island to which the legendary King Arthur, of Round Table fame, was carried after his last battle. It was ruled by the enchantress Morgan le Fay and her eight sisters, all skilled in healing. In 1921 the land on the northern peninsula was subdivided by Arthur J. Small. He appreciated the natural beauty of the district and stipulated there was to be no unnecessary destruction of the trees. One story says Small woke in the middle of the night declaring Avalon was to be the name for the subdivision. All the blocks of land in the subdivision were to have frontages of not less than 66 feet (20 metres) and a depth of 200 feet (60 metres), where possible. Small's house still stands in Bellevue Avenue, Avalon.

On 29 October 1827 John Farrell received a grant of 60 acres (24 hectares) at Pittwater which Therry's grants later adjoined. However, Avalon formed part of Father Therry's combined grants of 1833 and 1837 which stretched from Whale Beach to Newport and from the ocean to Pittwater and included Whale Beach, Careel Bay, Salt Pan, Clareville, Avalon and Bilgola. The land near Avalon Public School was for many years called Priest's Flat. Avalon was a tiny settlement of isolated farms and a few fishermen's cottages. Following the 1920s subdivision it was a holiday destination but by the 1930s permanent residents were settling around Avalon.

A famous 1890s Rugby Union player, Stanley Wickham, opened a store at Avalon and the first Post Office opened in his store on 15 May 1933. The next year money order facilities were provided but it was 1946 before the delivery of telegrams commenced at Avalon. Wickham's later became McDonald's and Bill McDonald, an old Avalon identity, claimed to have arrived in Avalon atop a load of goods his uncle brought to stock a small store. From the late 1930s until the 1950s le Clercq's had a general store on the north eastern corner of Old Barrenjoey Road and Avalon Parade. On his retirement from the ring Jimmy Carruthers, World Bantamweight Champion in 1952, ran a milk bar with his wife at Avalon.

Avalon Golf Club

Where Barrenjoey Road climbs from Avalon towards Bilgola Head and between Old Barrenjoey Road is the Avalon Golf Course. The south-east corner of the golf course is the location of Father Therry's controversial shaft for a coal mine. He is said to have employed a number of aged men to sink the shaft some 220 feet deep (67 metres). Guy Jennings[53] quotes Charles de Boos 'At no time have the men employed ever injured themselves by hard work.' On one occasion the overseer is said to have 'bolted with the month's pay of the men, and, not satisfied with that, took also the reverend father's horse,

though this was subsequently recovered, but only after paying a pretty stiffish sum for stabling expenses.'[54]

The golf club was originally private and formed by Arthur J. Small, the developer of Avalon in the 1920s. Small later subdivided some of the land but had a proviso that it remain accessible to the public. The course reverted to Warringah Shire Council following World War II and became a public course. The nine hole course remains a public course available to beginners and for games of social golf. There is also a Ladies' Club affiliated with the Ladies' Golf Union.

Angophora Reserve

Off Palmgrove Road at Avalon is The Pittwater Wildlife Sanctuary Angophora Reserve and Hudson Park covering 8 hectares.

Just within the entrance is a monument dedicated to Connie Adams (1933-1989) who devoted many years to preserving the natural beauty of the Avalon area.

The Angophora Reserve was originally purchased by the Wildlife Society in 1937 as a bushland sanctuary. The aim was to preserve a giant angophora tree and the reserve opened officially on 19 March 1938.

During the 1950-1960s the natural bush to the south and west of the reserve was subdivided. The larger area of Hudson Park was added to the original reserve.

The whole reserve has features of high conservation significance and is included on the Australian Heritage Commission's Register of the National Estate.

The angophora tree *(Angophora costata)* or Sydney red gum (also smooth barked apple) is a landscape item of historical significance. It is

claimed to be the oldest and largest of the species in the world. Although estimated to be only 30 to 35 metres tall it has a very thick trunk (10 metres circumference at the base). The foliage cover is now very sparse and the gnarled old broken branches make a pattern of smooth red limbs against the blue sky.

Bushland regeneration of the reserve has been carried out by the Warringah Shire Council and the National Trust of Australia (NSW).

A walking track winds through the reserve, where one can experience the peace and calm of the Australian bush and the gentle murmur of the breeze through the trees.

The reserve features areas of open forest and stands of cabbage tree palms. The palm stand in Hudson Park is about 0.5 hectares. The stand was once more extensive around the end of Ruskin Rowe but suffered with clearing and the overgrowth of lantana. About 500 square metres of fern swamp and a sedge swamp are also located in Hudson Park.

The reserve shelters frogs, lizards,

Two women pose in front of the giant Sydney red gum in the Angophora Reserve in 1938.

birds and eight species of mammals have been recorded in or near the reserve. Avalon's koala colony is the only example to persist within the suburbs. There may, however, be koalas within Davidson Park State Recreation Area. The koala's future does not appear promising. In 1970 it was estimated the colony numbered 123 plus, in 1989 perhaps only eight remained. The forested land on the peninsula has shrunk from 705 hectares (47% of the peninsula north of Bungan Beach) in 1946 to 125 hectares (8%) in 1989.

Also of importance within the reserve area are Aboriginal sites, one of the most archaeologically significant in the Sydney region. There is a burial site, shell midden and drawings. From one artefact it has been estimated the use of the shelter area may have commenced between 1500 to 2500 years ago, or even earlier.

Clareville

From Avalon shopping village the narrow two lane road twists endlessly above Pittwater. From Stokes Point the roadway links with Hudson Parade passing Paradise Beach and baths and Clareville Beach. There are tall spotted gums and the gardens are a riot of growth. Ruth Park says it is as 'secluded as bellbirds' nests'.[55]

Houses cling to the steep hillsides amid the sandstone outcrops and the native forest. By the turning roadside large fronds of fresh green bracken, sheltered by casuarinas, brush the bitumen. There are tall gums and clumps of tropical banana palms. Pittwater is blue like a Ken Done painting with the white splashes of moored boats, a purple tibouchina shrub flamboyant among the dull green gums of the foreshores and in a garden a clump of blue and orange strelitzia, the Bird of Paradise.

There are mud flats at Taylor's Point and the water sparkles between the gums, but Pittwater is not always sun and sparkling water. It has periods of torrential downpours when the distant hills appear as grey smudges and the rain splashes across the water's surface with a million jagged diagonals recalling the wild beauty of a distant Scottish loch.

On a hot summer's day the sun burns the foreshore rocks where the rowing boats are lined upended. The homes here are mostly elegant. Newcomers to the area may discover snakes and funnel web spiders lurking in the garden and there are also possums and bandicoots.

At the HMAS Penguin Diving School Annexe the long timber wharf stretches into Pittwater. The navy formerly had three torpedo targets north of the naval jetty on Taylor's Point spaced 1000 yards apart. The wharf seems an intrusion in this world of flashing water, cut like a diamond in the midday sun, the soft slap, slap of the lapping water at the shore and the white cumulus clouds massed behind the distant headlands.

Located 36 kilometres north of Sydney Clareville was also part of Therry's land grant. No one seems too sure of the derivation of the name Clareville. Frances Pollon[56] suggests the combination of Clare and ville may have come from an early home. Clareville has its own small secluded shopping area which includes The Belfry Antiques with eighteenth and early nineteenth century furniture, porcelain and silver.

Swiss born artist Sali Herman was a resident of Clareville. Born at Zurich in 1898 Herman came to Australia in 1937 and once lived at Rushcutters Bay on the harbour but in later life found Clareville. His son Ted and grand-daughter Nada Herman-Witkamp are also local artists. Artist Elaine Haxton was born in Melbourne and has lived in various locations around the world while pursuing her art career. For over forty years she has chosen to live at Clareville and her work 'From My Studio' captures its essence - spotted gum, the bushy grass tree plant with its sharp spear of minute flowers and the yachts, sails billowing, on the water.

Long Beach, 500 metres, faces across Pittwater and in the vicinity is a reserve area. The gardens of the houses are a riot of frangipani, shady jacaranda trees and large pink blowsy dahlias. In the peace and quietness of the very early morning there can be no more magical spot.

Bilgola Plateau

From Clareville the peninsula rises to Bilgola Plateau.

Bilgola is an Aboriginal name and Brian and Barbara Kennedy[57] suggest it may mean swirling water. The name was first used by James Meehan during one of his surveys. Meehan often used the Aboriginal name for particular districts and notes Belgoula in his journal of 6 May 1814. One version of the name's meaning is 'a pretty beach with steep slopes in the background studded with cabbage palms'. Although this is true, even today, of the oceanside Bilgola Beach it seems rather excessive.

In 1822 Robert Henderson (see p. 17) was granted one hundred acres of land and used the name Belgoola. Robert Henderson moved across Broken Bay to Brisbane Water to act as District Constable in 1824 but continued to graze cattle on his land. John Farrell (see p. 17) also grazed his cattle on Henderson's land, with permission and Farrell subsequently requested Governor Darling in 1826 to grant him Henderson's land. The magistrate who considered the request found Henderson had the better claim but in 1841 Henderson transferred 5 acres (2 hectares) to Farrell. Farrell used the name Belgoola.

William Bede Dalley (1831-1888) one time Attorney General and Acting Premier of New South Wales was another early resident of this district. He had built a castellated home at Manly named Marinella but dubbed Dalley's Castle by locals. Dalley, the son of convicts, gained some notoriety for sending New South Wales troops to the Sudan War in 1885, an action which caused a controversy akin to that of the Vietnam War in the 1960s. In the 1870s Dalley had a beach house named Bilgola House, a weatherboard residence with a dominant wooden tower sheltered by the native cabbage tree palms. In the twenties it was a guest house and visitors probably sat on the veranda sipping tea and gazing at the ocean. Bilgola Beach was then referred to as Dalley's Beach. It was also once called Mad Mick's Hollow and Cranky Alice's Beach for two elderly people who lived there and berated any children who happened to pass by.[58] Dalley's house was later owned by World War II aviator W. Oswald Watt who was awarded the Legion of Honour and Croix de Guerre by France. He died at the beach after apparently falling from the rocks. The house was later demolished.

Salt Pan Cove

From the heights of Bilgola Plateau the land plunges down to Pittwater. At certain points there are breathtaking views of the ocean and its beaches and Pittwater. The roads are steep and winding and as the plateau rushes down to Pittwater; the houses stand among the old forest where the sun slants on the trunks of the red gums. The shore is a series of curves and inlets such as Refuge Cove, South Beach and Salt Pan Cove. Salt was an important substance in our early days, required for salting meat and fish and curing hides. In this vicinity the seawater was held in an iron tank until condensed and the salt then used for commercial purposes.

Thirty acres (12 hectares) of the land around around Salt Pan and to the top of the escarpment[59] was a grant to James MacDonald. John Farrell was granted 60 acres (24 hectares) to the west of the Village Reserve.[60] John Farrell was an Irish convict transported in 1813 after having been found guilty of possessing an illegal bank note. Farrell prospered in the colony and owned land in Macquarie Street and a farm at Pittwater. It was Farrell's servant Tumey who alerted the authorities to the smuggling episode involving the *Fair Barbarian* (see page 17). Farrell died in 1851 and his Pittwater lands were inherited by his son, also John Farrell. Pittwater was a wild territory last century and the settlers were not always good neighbours. Farrell was involved in a case of disappearing cattle. Ten cows owned by James Therry, a nephew of the pioneer priest went missing and the remains of one was discovered on Farrell's property. Farrell was committed for trial and more of Therry's cattle vanished while Farrell was on bail. A youthful employee of Farrell informed to the police and Farrell was subsequently convicted and sentenced to seven years hard labour in 1864. Farrell apparently never served the sentence for in 1869 he was resident at

Manly Lagoon and the licensee of the new North Steyne Hotel in 1871. His Pittwater farms passed to his son, Johnny Farrell. From convict origins the Farrell family became respected citizens. They had a butchery on Manly's Corso and were proprietors of Manly's Colonnade Hotel, offering 'First-Class Accommodation'.[61] Johnny Farrell died in 1933. Considering property values around Salt Pan Cove in the 1990s one wonders what Johnny Farrell would make of it. In 1925 he purchased 45 acres (18 hectares) for £3000.

Tiny Florence Park on Salt Pan Cove is a restful spot with golden autumn trees and views to the boats, wharves and deep blue ridged hills. Familiarity it is said breed contempt but it is doubtful if one could ever tire of the Pittwater views. From Salt Pan Cove and Salt Pan Point the view is to Pittwater's only island, Scotland Island (see p 65). Overseas visitors who venture this far from the city discover this beautiful area is a well kept secret.

Royal Motor Yacht Club

The Royal Motor Yacht Club commands a magnificent position with moorings on Horseshoe Cove. The Royal Motor Yacht Club at Rose Bay on Sydney Harbour dates from 1910 and the Pittwater Club was formed in 1926. This followed a visit to the United States of America by the Commodore of the Motor Boat Club of New South Wales, Rose Bay (the club's original name), Stuart F. Doyle. He had noted the United States' clubs had branch clubs in adjacent areas. Broken Bay was selected as the site for the branch club and finally Horseshoe Cove on Pittwater chosen as the most suitable site for the erection of a clubhouse, boatshed and slipway. The club numbered 90 members but as road access was difficult, a dirt track impassable in

wet weather, building supplies were shipped in by water.

The new clubhouse opened officially on 17 March 1928. During the 1926/1927 season King George V granted the privilege of the use of 'Royal' to the parent club at Rose Bay and it became the Royal Motor Yacht Club of New South Wales.

The original clubhouse at Pittwater built close to the seawall was destroyed by fire in 1935 but the new building was opened by the year's end on 14 December.

Over the years the club was able to purchase further land and increased its water frontage to approximately 147 metres. During the period of World War II many sizeable cruisers were confiscated by the Royal Australian Navy and used by the Naval Auxiliary Patrol. Petrol rationing had in any case suspended boating as a pleasurable pastime for the duration of the war.

After the war the Royal Motor Yacht Club took stock, facilities were improved and extensions to the buildings made. A swimming pool opened in 1959 and was later remodelled as the club continued to grow with active members and more reconstruction.

In 1966 a new club house was built around the old clubhouse and was officially opened on 17 August 1968 by the wife of the New South Wales Governor, Lady Cutler.

With the passing years boating has increased in popularity and there has been an even greater demand for marina berths, dry storage and moorings. In 1980 the Royal Motor Yacht Club opened a new western marina complex with 103 berths. In all the club provides berths for almost 200 boats.

Early known as a 'family club' where members could relax, swim and boat with their families the club also offers its members a wide variety of activities including sailing, fishing, cruise competition, cruising safaris and game fishing.

A portion of this area was once named Glen Melville for Robert Melville who was granted 60 acres (24 hectares) from Horseshoe Cove to roughly the middle of Crystal Bay.

Newport

Newport spans the peninsula from the ocean to Pittwater. The coastal region has bluff Bungan Head with its celebrated castle built by Albert Albers in 1919 from sandstone quarried on the site. Albers, a German art dealer, arrived in Australia in 1880 when he was fourteen years of age. In 1918 driving a sulky in the region he found Bungan Head and on the beach drew in the sand a plan for his castle. At first only at weekends, Albers lived in his castle from 1944 until his death in 1959. Part of Bungan Head is still marked on street directories as Bushrangers Hill and no doubt runaway convicts and cattle duffers hid here in the early days. This lofty site provided them with a commanding view from which they could see the law approaching from a great distance. There would have been little chance of the authorities locating them in the wild and isolated territory. Maybanke Anderson[62] claims the bushrangers were two convict servants to James Jenkins, who ran away from his homestead and lived in this area under an overhang of rock. Their crime was petty pilfering. A local Aborigine reported them to the authorities and they ended up in gaol. Mrs. Anderson states the Aborigine was known as Black Bowen and was one of six local Aborigines taken to California about 1848 by Richard Hill at the time of the American gold rushes. Black Bowen was the only survivor of the trip, his compatriots died and he declared of North America, 'No wood for fire, but plenty cold wind, and plenty, plenty water.'[63]

A Public Auction of the Bushranger Hill estate was held on 19 January 1917.

Newport Beach and the beach reserve is crowded at week ends with young surfers revelling in the sun, the sand and the surf. The local shops are worth exploring and the bibliophile will spend hours at Dial-a-Book crammed from floor to ceiling with a fascinating array of pre-loved books.

Newport was in fact a new port for coastal steamers in the latter part of the nineteenth century. Newport itself was a popular destination for day trippers who arrived by steamer with loaded picnic baskets to enjoy a day at the seaside. Today with its peaceful atmosphere it is hard to imagine the suburb as a busy port with vessels being unloaded at its wharf in Pittwater. Four steamers ran weekly and the wharf survived until 1902.

Unfortunately the Pushes, gangs of unruly larrikins who terrorised inner Sydney at the turn of the century, also discovered the joys of a steamer trip to Newport. There were fights between rival groups and often drunken brawls, for illegal liquor was distilled around Pittwater and the police were far away at Manly. The local residents were far from impressed by this behaviour every Sunday and decided to take the law into their own hands. The manager of the Newport Hotel, Tom Hodges (also Odges, Odgers), happened to be an ex-policeman and he hired an American boxer, Jack Castlemaine. The two men enlisted the help of a local, David Scott from Scott's boarding house, and he hired two more boxers. When the paddle steamer *City of Grafton* was moored at the wharf on St Valentine's Day,

Sunday 14 February 1892, Hodges and his men were waiting. Once again the larrikins sauntered off the steamer to be met by two of the boxers stripped to the waist ready for battle. The gangs charged the men, denuded a nearby orchard and pelted Scott's boarding house with fruit and rocks. They were jubilant by the time they reached the Newport Hotel but Hodges had had enough. As the larrikins smashed glasses and started to wreck the hotel the manager and his bouncer attacked the gang, supported to the rear by the two boxers who had raced up with pieces of four by two timber. The Battle of Newport raged until the ferry departed two hours later with the pushes vowing vengeance the next week. The following Sunday the rowdies, after a rough passage to Pittwater, mostly stayed on board rather than face the heroes of Newport again. After that Newport lost its appeal for the Sydney pushes.

A watercolour by H. Brees of Bolton's Farm and the Pittwater Church of England, 1860.

Robert Campbell, a nephew of the famous merchant received the first land grant at Newport, part of 700 acres (283 hectares) granted on 31 August 1819.[64] But the Farrells (see p. 43) are seen as the pioneers of Newport. On 6 July 1833 John Farrell received 60 acres (24 hectares) at Newport Beach and on 13 January 1842 30 acres (12 hectares) at Little Reef, Newport. The family history is entwined with the history of Newport and with the Manly area. The beach at Newport was once Farrell's Beach.

An old newspaper advertisement of 1919 advised the auction of the 'beautiful seaside resort, the Newport Hotel. A popular, up-to-date House, so easy of access to the city by regular motor service.'[65] It was then part of the estate of the late William Boulton. The Boultons were early Newport residents, William having come across to the Pittwater peninsula from the gold-fields of Kalgoorlie in the 1870s. There is mention of 'Bolton's Farm' in the 1880 publication *'Description of Newport. Pittwater and Hawkesbury Lakes.'* [66]

'About a mile beyond Narabeen (sic) the road crosses a steep hill from the top of which the hills beyond Newport, as well as Lord Loftus Point, are distinctly visible, we come next to Boltons Farm the subject of an illustration. The soil of this locality is very rich, and it is rather strange that it is not cultivated.'

Boulton had become the licensee of the Newport Hotel in 1887. The hotel was earlier owned by Charles Jeanneret (later Mayor of Hunters Hill and one time manager of the Parramatta River Steam Company) and George Pile. Jeanneret had been one of the party at the foundation laying ceremony at Barrenjoey Lighthouse and was the owner of *The Florrie* which carried the party

Lord Loftus Point and Scotland Island from the Newport Hotel as drawn by H. Brees.

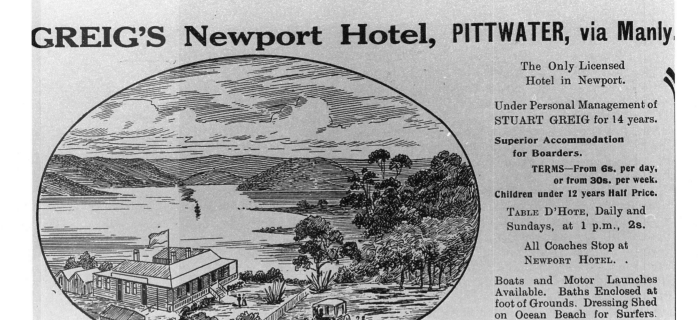

GREIG'S Newport Hotel, PITTWATER, via Manly

The Only Licensed
Hotel in Newport.

Under Personal Management of
STUART GREIG for 14 years.

**Superior Accommodation
for Boarders.**

TERMS—From 6s. per day,
or from 30s. per week.
Children under 12 years Half Price.

TABLE D'HOTE, Daily and
Sundays, at 1 p.m., 2s.

All Coaches Stop at
NEWPORT HOTEL. .

Boats and Motor Launches
Available. Baths Enclosed at
foot of Grounds. Dressing Shed
on Ocean Beach for Surfers.

Greig's Catering is noted
:: as Best in the District. ::

STUART GREIG, Proprietor.

View of Newport, with Hotel in foreground.

The Newport Hotel when Stuart Grieg was the proprietor.

to Barrenjoey. The *Sydney Morning Herald*[67] states 'On the opposite side of the bay is Newport the property of Messrs. Mills & Pile and Mr. Jeanneret, who are erecting an hotel, for the accommodation of visitors to the bay. It will have a fine situation....'

Boulton later leased the hotel to William Buflin, who arrived in Sydney in 1866 from Ireland and had been the licensee of a hotel in Wharf Street, Sydney. The Boultons, however owned the hotel until it was sold in 1919 to the brewery firm, Reschs Ltd.

An early watercolour illustration by H. Brees[68] depicts the simple hotel building standing in an almost English parkland setting. It is single storeyed with numerous doors opening onto a veranda supported by wooden posts. The land had once been part of the Bassett Darley Estate, so named because after Captain Darley's death in 1864, his widow Katherine (nee Wentworth) married a squatter, William T.

Bassett. In the early 1900s the hotel was enclosed with a picket fence and a wooden sign over the gateway declaring 'Newport Hotel. Table d'hote 1 o'clock'.

The hotel was once 'the pub with no beer'. Charles Swancott[69] writes that due to heavy rain at Newport the publican ran out of beer. He borrowed a horse and cart and set off for Manly where he purchased twelve dozen bottles of beer. On the return trip he broke an axle on Bushrangers Hill and lost ten dozen bottles of his load. The smashed bottles were still by the roadside in 1938.

Following the sale of the Newport Hotel to Reschs Ltd the old building was demolished and a new brick hotel built. Time removed the Scotch fir tree, trellis of grapes, quince trees and kitchen garden. Remodelled in 1954 the hotel was damaged in a fire on 30 August 1967. The present hotel, rebuilt in 1971, has a history dating back to the early days of Newport.

Perhaps the old licensees of earlier years would be happy to know a Newport Hotel still overlooks Pittwater.

In 1905 Newport's population numbered only 100 and even in 1925 an old photograph shows scattered settlement and Bungan Castle prominent on the distant headland.

The old families of the Farrells, the Boultons, the Buflins, who ran the local store, the Scotts and their boarding house, Kempsey born Jack Miles of 'The Avenue - Newport.

Engineer & Boat Builder'[70] and the Solomon Brothers, George, Herb and Fred who had a boatshed on Old Mangrove Bay are half forgotten memories.

Today there is a tropical lushness to Newport. Tall umbrella palms are silhouetted against the blue sky, hibiscus shrubs flaunt their vivid pink flowers along the suburban streets, the cicadas drone ceaselessly in the summer heat and the waters of Pittwater appear and disappear among the houses and the trees.

The Newport Hotel was a rest point for travellers in the 1900s.

Royal Prince Alfred Yacht Club

On Pittwater at Green Point is the Royal Prince Alfred Yacht Club.

The club is named for Queen Victoria's son, Prince Alfred, Duke of Edinburgh, on whom an assassination attempt was made at Clontarf, Middle Harbour during a royal visit in 1868.

The club's origins possibly date back to the Mosquito Yacht Club which was already active in 1856. In 1867 the name was changed to the Prince Alfred Yacht Club. Some claim the Mosquito Club was Australia's first sailing club although Australia's first yacht club is the Tamar Yacht Club, Launceston, Tasmania founded in 1837. The Mosquito Club met in McGrath's Hotel, King Street, Sydney; the Prince Alfred Yacht Club was to meet in rooms at Campagnoni's in Pitt Street and at the Hotel Australia before acquiring

The Duke of Edinburgh visits the Royal Prince Alfred Yacht Club in 1968. The club was named for an earlier Duke of Edinburgh.

club rooms in Bull's Chambers in what is now Martin Plaza. From these landlocked premises the club's business was discussed and members sailed on the harbour in magnificent yachts with the huge sails of an earlier era. Easter Camps were held at the Basin on Pittwater in 1907. F.J. Jackson made his residence here available to members.

By 1919 inspections were made of land at Green Point, Newport and a report dated 9 October 1919 states:

'Of all the pieces of land inspected, that piece known as Green Point immediately across from Scott's Boarding House at Newport, commends itself to your sub-committee as being eminently suitable as a site for a clubhouse. The area is 1 acre, 1 rood, 22 poles and its situation is excellent, being prominent and lending itself to display such as a progressive club like our own is entitled to. It has deep waterfrontage to the Bay.'[71]

By 20 October 1919 the committee was authorised to buy the land at Pittwater for £650.

A flag pole, the mast of the *Bona*, was erected. By 1924 a shed

stood on the site and the sites for moorings were agreed upon. Members though were slow to move their vessels to Pittwater. At one stage there was even discussion about selling the Pittwater property. It was not until 17 December 1938 that the Pittwater Club House was opened by the New South Wales Governor, Lord Wakehurst. The club house was in fact the boatshed and the Pittwater sailing season opened on 29 September 1939 just 26 days after the declaration of World War II. The club was closed on 18 March 1942 due to the war. Vessels were removed from Pittwater, some taken by the Royal Australian Navy and small boats hidden at Berowra Waters and Cowan Creek.

It was not until 1946 that the RPAYC was able to surge ahead. In 1959 the club acquired an adjoining property, Moonbar, for new club rooms and provision was made for a junior sailing division. By 1968 the Royal Prince Alfred Yacht Club was engaged in the most extensive yachting activity in New South Wales. In that year the Duke of Edinburgh was to lay the foundation stone of a new club house this seemed appropriate since an earlier Duke of Edinburgh had lent his name to the Club. However a 60 knot nor-westerly blew down the flagpole and the facilities for the ceremony. The Duke said he would lay the stone by remote control and member Jack Gale lowered the stone to its foundation.

For many years the Club's headquarters had been located in 39 Rowe Street, that once fascinating and colourful corner of the city flanked by the Hotel Australia (once the site of Starkey's ginger beer factory). On 30 October 1972 the headquarters transferred to Green Point. In its long history the club has collected much memorabilia and, of course, many rich and beautiful trophies.

The Royal Prince Alfred Yacht Club holds an important place in the history of Australian yachting and in

Pittwater's history and mindful of this fact the club has produced its own history *Yachting and the Royal Prince Alfred Yacht Club* by Graeme Norman, a keen yachtsman and former Lieutenant-Commander, Royal Australian Navy.

Between the Royal Motor Yacht Club and the Royal Prince Alfred Yacht Club there are heavily timbered hills where the houses overlook Pittwater and the roadway continues to Crystal Bay.

Lord and Lady Wakehurst touring Pittwater on their visit in 1938.

Crystal Bay

The name Crystal Bay immediately gives the image of crystal clear waters but it is a quiet backwater and at low tide there are sandy flats. Scotts Old Fashioned Hotel once overlooked Crystal Bay. Horse coaches operated from Manly to the hotel and usually the journey took one and a half hours from Sydney. Scotts hired launches and provided hamper lunches for picnickers. Today yachts dominate the area for the moorings and facilities of the Royal Prince Alfred Yacht Club are on Green Point. There is a tiny reserve area and the homes bordering the bay have green lawns to the foreshore.

Haystack Point

The southern arm of Crystal Bay is Haystack Point and is said to derive its name from a curious occurrence.[72] The Hawkesbury River has always been prone to flooding and the year 1873 witnessed a major flood. A haystack from a Hawkesbury farm fastened to a framework of large logs was carried by the floodwaters down the Hawkesbury and borne by tide and wind into Pittwater. The travelling haystack drifted to the area beyond Crystal Bay and it was thereafter Haystack Point. It was said several pigs had travelled on the haystack during its long journey and they were recovered by a local fisherman from Mona Vale.

Tiny Dearin Park overlooks Heron Cove and the foreshore sneaks around to Old Mangrove Bay. Those fortunate to live overlooking the water enjoy the solitude of their quiet arm of Pittwater.

From Bushrangers Hill Governor Phillip and three of his party had gazed this way to Pittwater at dusk one August day in 1788[73] noting Pittwater extending from Winji Jimmi to Church Point. During the trek in the space of half a mile they collected 'twenty-five flowers of plants and shrubs of different genera and species, specimens of which I have transmitted to Mr. Wilson, particularly the Red Gum Tree.'[74] They would surely not have dreamed of the eventual spread of settlement and Pittwater sprinkled with hundreds of pleasure craft.

The explorers set off the next day to visit the area of Bayview and explored a creek. J.S.N. Wheeler[75] records this creek as Shaw's Creek, Bayview which originated in a swamp 'known one hundred years ago as Winneremy'.[76] A Lands Department map later marked it as Winni Jenny. Across Old Mangrove Bay is Winji Jimmi Reserve, probably a corruption of the original Winneremy. The reserve is located at the end of a point and there are boats on Pittwater and views to the houses on the hillsides. The streets here are lined with modern comfortable homes and Mona Street leads to Pittwater High School and Pittwater Road.

Pittwater High School

The first little Pittwater School was built in 1888, Australia's centenary year. It became Bayview Public School in 1892. Maybanke Anderson who was to deliver her paper 'The Story of Pittwater' to the Royal Australian Historical Society in 1920 used to treat the local school children to ripe grapes from her garden. Mrs. Anderson lived close to the Bayview Post Office. Maybanke Susannah Anderson (1845-1927) arrived in Sydney with her family in 1855. She was deserted by her first husband and established a school in Sydney. She later married Professor Anderson of the University of Sydney. She was a feminist and active in various organisations in Sydney. In the early 1900s Pittwater children travelled to the school by the motor boat *Patonga*. The school closed on 7 September 1906 when a new school opened at nearby Mona Vale.

The rather utilitarian Pittwater High School is surrounded by soft casuarinas, melaleucas, other native shrubs and hibiscus. Students wander across the grounds loaded with bulging backpacks of school books.

Before the school was built there were mangrove swamps and the area was reclaimed and filled with seabeach sand. The school opened in 1963, under the headmastership of Mr. Gorral, with 220 pupils in six class groups and a small staff of ten full time and two part time teachers. The reclamation and the initial buildings cost some $800,000 but at first the school coped with improvised rooms and facilities.

The first edition of the school magazine *Kalori* appeared in 1963 and in a later issue (1966) a student remembered the first day at Pittwater High. The day was 'terribly wet', only one building was finished and that without plaster to the walls. Students walked on boards to the barn.

In 1965 a school newspaper *Nunana Kalori* 'little message stick' was produced, in addition to the school magazine.

The sixties was the era of Vietnam protests and in 1966 *Kalori* included a letter signed by several students in which they asked, 'Will Australia be able to overcome her new found role of intruder and aggressor?'

By February 1966 there were 974 pupils in 28 class groups. The Department of Education was asked to provide a total staff of 45, including five subject masters.

Perhaps unusual in a suburban school, Pittwater High is some 30 kilometres from Sydney, is the Agricultural Department. The subject is an elective for Years 8, 9 and 10. During the junior years it is a basic course but taught in more depth for the senior years, Years 11 and 12. The students care for sheep, pigs, geese and chickens. The eggs are sold as is the honey produced from the department's bees. There is also an agricultural plot for plants and the study of agricultural methods.

Pittwater High was also one of the first schools to offer Student Driver Education courses.

Not so successful was the building of the Bini Shell, a new concept in school architecture rather resembling a grounded flying saucer, as the school auditorium. The dome of the shell collapsed on 5 August 1986 and a school cleaner was injured. A few years earlier a similar dome had collapsed at Canley Vale school. On 8 August there was a teacher walkout following a finding of asbestos in the rubble of the collapsed dome.

With the school located close to Pittwater it is not perhaps surprising that in *Kalori* (1968) it was reported that sailing was 'introduced half-way through last summer.' Mr. Vick had been the instigator of the scheme and during the summer of '68 the school had over thirty boats racing, ranging from M.J.s to 16 foot skiffs (48 metres). A well-known yachtsman, Zachary Stollznow ran classes for all 'school boys'[77] on Tuesday afternoons. The first class had twelve students who were taught the basic fundamentals of sailing and the class was to be competently sailing in six weeks. Stollznow prevailed on De Havilland to lend a boat to the school for classes. The course was so successful it was decided 'that even girls are now allowed to try their hand so long as they have a boat.'[78]

It was a natural progression for the school to aim for their own yacht and on Monday 9 March 1970 the *Kalori* was launched at the Royal Prince Alfred Yacht Club at Newport. The ceremony was attended by the New South Wales Governor Sir Roden Cutler and his wife, Lady Cutler launched the *Kalori*. The maroon, grey and white hulled vessel slid down the slipway, its sails quickly hoisted and *Kalori* moved out across Pittwater.

The school did not neglect its more normal curriculum and there are many famous 'old boys and girls'.

NIDA trained actor Tom Burlinson was School Captain in 1983. His family home was at Mona Vale and he grew up around Bayview and Bilgola. Burlinson's acting career commenced at Pittwater High when he played in a production of 'My Fair Lady'. He went on to star in the film 'The

Man from Snowy River'. Chef and restaurateur Anders Ousbach is another 'name', as is rugby union player Peter Phelps. Trumpeter James Morrison still resides in the area. Rock star Johnny O'Keefe's children attended the school as did those of former Seekers member Keith Pottinger and the daughters of writer Tom Keneally.

Mona Vale / Bayview

Peter Patullo once held land in this vicinity and in 1821 (the last year of Macquarie's governorship of the colony) built a house near the south east corner of Pittwater where Bayview Golf Links are now located.[79] In 1832 he was granted 80 acres (32 hectares) of land by Governor Bourke on condition that thirty acres (12 hectares) were cleared and cultivated or buildings or fencing erected to the value of £150. It was surveyed by Surveyor J. Larmer. Larmer also surveyed other Pittwater farms including those of Jeremiah Bryant, 8 acres (3 hectares) and Robert McIntosh, Snr., 200 acres (81 hectares and Robert McIntosh, Jnr., 40 acres (16 hectares).

A track wound its way around the Bayview farms. Coaches carried travellers to the famous Rock Lily Inn, Mona Vale built in 1886 where

The Rock Lily Hotel in the busy 1890s.

Leon Houreaux, a huge man of around 125 kilos, looked after the travellers and found time to grow his own grapes at the rear of his establishment. At the Rock Lily passengers changed coaches, the large coach continuing to Bayview and Church Point and a smaller one carrying on to Newport. At one period Bayview began to out-pace Newport but in time Newport with its wharf and steamer service became more populous and Bayview slipped back to quieter obscurity. The horses, coaches and sulkies that once crowded the road in front of the Rock Lily Inn have gone as indeed have the native rock lilies after which Houreaux named his inn but the old building survives as the modern traffic ceaselessly flows along Pittwater Road.

At the road junction at Mona Vale, Barrenjoey Road heads out to the peninsula while Pittwater Road leads to Bayview and Church Point. Just past Mona Vale shopping area is a home of an earlier era. Dungarvon is the oldest complete masonry and stone home on the Pittwater Peninsula. The land here was subdivided in 1887 and in 1897 the house was built by Samuel Stringer. Stringer brought masons out from England to construct the house. One of Stringer's daughters, Lilian May, married Frederick Oliver of the Pittwater pioneering family.

Close to this house is St John's Anglican Church also built of fine stone in 1906/1907. A wooden church of St John the Baptist was erected overlooking Bongin Bongin Beach, Mona Vale, (also known as Cedar Log Beach) in 1871 above Boulton's farm. Because the inhabitants were moving from the area it was decided to relocate the church and it was conveyed by a bullock team to a new site on Bay View Road in the area of Winneremy. Some pioneers had been buried in the graveyard around the old church and with the church's removal the graves were neglected and then forgotten. Its site was relocated by Mr. P.W. Gledhill, then

President of the Manly Warringah and Pittwater Historical Society, Mr. C.R. Stoddard and Mr. J.J. Shaw of Mona Vale. Mr. Stoddard, a surveyor, used an old photograph in the Mitchell Library to relocate the site of the original church. An investigation of the area led to a discovery of a portion of a sand-stone headstone which proved to be that of Annie Priscilla Wilson, aged two years. Another headstone belonged to a blacksmith, Frederick William Stark, who died at Barrenjoey on 16 February 1881 at the age of 27 years. He was one of the workers on the Barrenjoey Lighthouse. The recovered head-stones were placed in the grounds of St John's at Mona Vale.

The church, after which Church Point was named, was demolished in 1938.

55

Bayview Golf Club

The golfers follow the balls across the green sward of Bayview Golf Course. This land was a portion of the area known as the Winnereremy Swamp and the story of how it evolved into the golf club is interesting.

A New Zealand sheep farmer named Orr and his wife visited the locality about 1920 and were impressed by what they viewed. Orr purchased 43.5 acres (17.6 hectares) of land which had been owned earlier by Robert McIntosh, Senior. McIntosh Senior was a member of the 46th Regiment of Foot (the South Devons), the regiment which replaced Governor Macquarie's 73rd Highlanders. He was appointed Chief Constable for the area from North Harbour to Broken Bay in 1819. To confuse matters his son, Robert McIntosh Junior, also held 40 acres at Mona Vale.

The Orrs built a house and ran some sheep on the land. Both were keen golfers and the green flat cropped area allowed them to play a game. Locals asked to be allowed to play on the six hole course and gradually a small group of people played regularly. Probably more as a joke one player nailed a box to a tree labelled 'GREEN FEES, 2/-'. Mrs. Orr provided tea for the players and a wooden hut was built as a tea shelter. A small brick club house followed. After her husband's death in 1942 Mrs. Orr leased the course and club house privately and the beginnings of a private club formed. It was constituted as Bayview Golf Club on 10 December 1948. As the club grew in numbers all the Orr land was purchased in 1967. By that time the club house required extensions and the original small wooden tea hut served for many years as a 'half way house'. The club has approximately 600 members and the course is 18 holes with a Par of 70. No golf club could have a more homely origin and on a crisp autumn day the course is picturesque with its many casuarinas, cabbage tree palms and melaleucas fringing the course.

The golf course is bordered on one side by Cabbage Tree Road named for the indigenous tall palms. A botanist named Ellis is quoted in 1895 as saying 'It is to be hoped that these beautiful specimens of a fast disappearing and interesting class of plants may be long spared from destruction'.[80]

Here in Cabbage Tree Road Sir Edward Hallstrom had a farm and grew crops for the animals at Taronga Zoo. Hallstrom, an industrialist, maker of the Silent Knight refrigerator, and a philanthropist was appointed a trustee of the zoo in 1941. He became Chairman of the Zoo's Board in 1949 and Honorary Life Director on his retirement in 1967.

The name Bayview is self explanatory and was officially adopted on 21 August 1882 when a post office was opened on a farm owned by the Collins family. The farm covered 80 acres (32 hectares) and the family had moved to the area from Careel Bay. A daughter, Katherine May Collins, became the first post mistress and married a local man, J.J. Roche. Roche was remembered as 'a sturdy squatter type with a Victorian beard' by J.S.N. Wheeler[81]. Collins had a large orchard growing oranges, lemons, peaches, plums, apricots, guavas and loquats. The family made fine fruit jams and also had a good poultry farm.

Once Bayview was a district of farms and orchards. No doubt it was a hard life but with a rustic charm. There were the shell collectors and the shingle makers, splitting the local timber to make the wooden roofing shingles carried to Sydney by local ships. Local timber was also cut and transported to Sydney as firewood.

Bayview Wharf, close to the Post Office, was not constructed

Bayview House as seen from Lord Loftus Point at Newport, photographed by Henry King.

Residents of Bayview House, overlooking Pittwater in the 1880s.

until 1901 by the New South Wales Department of Works. It was passed to the control of the Warringah Shire Council in 1906. Maybanke Anderson[82] claimed in the 1920s the southern shore of Pittwater was sinking and at the wharf casuarinas which once stood fifteen metres from high water then stood on the verge of the bay.

Part of McIntosh's land grant was later sold to a man named McKeown and cut into small blocks and the area named Sunnyside.

At the turn of the century Bayview had a brickworks located on Taylor's Flat operated by J. Austin and an associate named James Symonds. There were kilns and drying sheds and the business was probably kept busy in this locality for the other closest brickworks were at Brookvale.

The winding road leads past Rowland Reserve, a well kept park area, the 1st Bayview Sea Scout Group boatshed, Gibson Marina, Bayview where hire boats are available seven days a week and Bayview Anchorage. In this world of yachts, boats and water there is a small school.

Bayview from Newport Wharf as it looked in 1918.

Loquat Valley Anglican Preparatory School, Bayview

This small school stands on a portion of the land granted to Robert McIntosh. P. Taylor built a house on the land in 1894 and in time it passed to his son, the aviator Sir Gordon Taylor. It was Taylor, who with Kingsford Smith, while attempting to inaugurate a mail service between Australia and New Zealand in the *Southern Cross,* in 1935 climbed out under the 'plane's wing on several occasions to transfer oil from one engine to another when the 'plane developed engine trouble.

Sir Gordon Taylor had some original ideas on education and he selected the location of and established the Loquat Valley School in 1947. Mrs. Day was the School's first Headmistress with thirteen pupils, two of them Taylor's daughters. Mrs. Day purchased the school later in 1947 and it was only ill-health in 1967 that forced her to consider closing it. The Sydney Church of England Girls' Grammar School (SCEGGS) purchased the school that year and appointed Mrs. L. Prescott as Headmistress. The school caters for children from kindergarten to Year 6 and has 187 pupils. On 6 May 1992 it celebrated its 45th birthday.

Pittwater Road

Modern homes line Pittwater Road and prominent residents such as Sir Rupert Clarke, Sydney Snow of the Sydney store and Sir Roy McCaughey once owned homes here. The latter's house, on the waterfront was later owned by the noted yachtsman Sir Bill Northam, who became an Olympic yachtsman in 1965. Northam, in his yacht *Barranjoey* (a variation of the headland's name), won a Gold Medal for the International 5.5 Metre Class at the Olympic Games in Tokyo that year. The win meant the *Barranjoey* was awarded the World Championship of the class. The Gold Cup was on display at the Royal Prince Alfred Yacht Club for a period.

The famous theatrical stars Googie Withers and husband John McCallum have enjoyed Pittwater for years and their children attended the Loquat Valley School.

One house evoked the wrath of Melbourne architect, Robin Boyd, in 1960 when he wrote

'The really depressing parts of Sydney, however, are in the North Shore Executive Zone. Here some of the most dramatically beautiful country available to suburban commuters anywhere in the world seems to draw out a delinquent streak in nearly everyone who builds. Out through French's Forest and along the spine above Pittwater one can find three or four of the most notable modern houses in Australia. They are nationally, and to an extent internationally, known by their photographs. But the photographs do not show their neighbours. The few thoughtful buildings of the area are all but lost in a wild scramble of outrageous Featurism clearly planned for the express purpose of extracting a gasp of envy from each passing sports car. By the placid water's edge of the most charmingly tranquil home-building sites one could imagine, is a structure of multitudinous angles and rainbows of colour which exemplifies the assault on the North Shore.'[83] With the passing years the colours of this home near Loquat Valley School have somewhat mellowed.

The road to Church Point is a world of water and sunshine, mangroves and mud flats, boats and boating. The Bayview Yacht Racing Association headquarters have a commanding view over the wide open bay. The road was surveyed by G.S. Cheeney in 1877.

J.S.N. Wheeler wrote,'Bayview has always been famous for its Spotted Gums growing on the roadside. The grown trees are thirty and forty feet in the barrels, with bark of yellow-green shade.'[84] In the late 1970s the National Trust of Australia (NSW) expressed concern about the trees stating the spotted gums (Eucalyptus maculata) of Church Point and Bayview are some of the finest in Sydney. The Trust opposed the widening of the road and recommended that 'the inhabited shores of Pittwater should be "an area of special urban and historic significance".'[85] The Trust noted the Warringah Shire Council had delineated a 'foreshore scenic protection area' on its planning scheme map. The aim of the designation was to encourage private dwellings to meet certain aesthetic standards in order to maintain the existing visual quality. The Trust agreed that the southern shoreline at Bayview was the main access feasible for Sydney people. The access should be retained, 'but we would want it Beautiful'. [86]

Church Point

This area has always been noted for its beauty and the road curves from Bayview onto Church Point beside Phillip's 'finest piece of water' dazzling in the sun with the white hulled yachts bobbing on the surface.

Few of the many who visit Church Point are aware of the derivation of its name and that just across the road from the wharf and store the remnants of an old cemetery remain where the pioneers sleep quietly above the blue waters of Pittwater.

Church services were once held under the loquat trees where the Bayview Post Office later stood. George McIntosh and William Henry McKeown were anxious for a church to be built. The church came about when pioneer, William Oliver, gave the Methodist Church one acre of ground for ten shillings on the proviso a church would be built soon thereafter. The little wooden church was built in 1872 at the cost of 60 pounds and it stood on the hillside among the tall gums until its demolition in April 1932. McKeown, one of the instigators of the church, gave a saddle horse to bring the preacher to the services. The simple church boasted a manual pedal organ, ornate pulpit and coconut matting covering the wooden floor. Among the parishioners were the Misses Woods who, dressed in long white dresses and shady hats, sailed across from Lovett Bay in their sixteen foot sailing boat.

At one period the area was known as Chapel Point.

Amongst the few old remaining headstones are some of the Oliver family - Mary Oliver Died July 12 1870 Aged 65 Years. William Oliver Died May 10 1882 Aged 75 Years. Thomas Albert Oliver Died 7 February 1918 Aged 75 Years.

The first Oliver in Sydney appears to have been Henry Oliver who was granted land in the district of Hunters Hill at Lane Cove, now part of Killara, in 1814. By the 1828 Census he held 45 acres (18 hectares), later inherited and then mortgaged by his son, William. William married in 1830 at St James' Church in Sydney and his wife Mary had fourteen children. William became a mounted policeman and a bailiff but by 1836 was the landlord of the Sawyers' Arms at Lane Cove and also operated a bakery - a man of many talents. At Pittwater he discovered a forest of red oak and acquired 30 acres (12 hectares) at Elvina Bay. The timber

Rugged sandstone cliffs and lonely beaches fringe the coastline of Pittwater Peninsula. To the right of centre lies Scotland Island, Pittwater's only island. (Boats Afloat)

Left:
*Nature and time have
sculpted Barrenjoey
Headland. (Susan Wright)*

Opposite page:
Top:
*Sunshine and shadow across
the face of Barrenjoey
headland seen from Palm
Beach. Barrenjoey
lighthouse is etched against
the clouds. (Susan Wright)*

Opposite page:
Bottom:
*Lion Island crouches like its
namesake in Broken Bay.
(Catherine Warne)*

Above:
The sand spit which ties
Barrenjoey to the
mainland is washed by the
ocean and Pittwater.
(Susan Wright)

Right:
Palm Beach at Pittwater as
the sun sets behind Coasters
Retreat. (Susan Wright)

The Angophora costata
*(smooth-barked apple) with
its glowing rusty-red bark is
native to Pittwater.
(Susan Wright)*

Left:
Family boating on Station (Barrenjoey) Beach which curves to Barrenjoey headland and its lighthouse. (Rob Jenson)

Opposite page:
Top:
Church Point ferries take visitors around Pittwater. (Susan Wright)

Opposite page:
Bottom:
Lunching at La Palma, Barrenjoey House, Palm Beach. (Rob Jenson)

Left:
Telopea speciosissima (Waratah), found in the Ku-Ring-Gai Chase National Park, is native to the coast and Great Dividing Range. It is the NSW floral emblem. (Susan Wright)

Top:
Tranquillity at dusk on Saltpan Cove. (Susan Wright)

Above:
Palm Beach is Pittwater's favourite windsurfing spot. (Susan Wright)

Left:
Pittwater's ferry wharfs provide a lot of recreational fun. (Rob Jenson)

Opposite page:
Looking north from Bilgola Plateau to Taylors Point. (Susan Wright)

Above:
A little piece of paradise at
Coasters Retreat.
(Catherine Warne)

Above right:
Rainbow lorikeets are
welcome visitors to local
gardens.
(Susan Wright)

Right:
The superbly sited Palm
Beach Golf Club was
founded in 1924.
(Catherine Warne)

McCarrs Creek — bushland, fishing and solitude. (Susan Wright)

Houses bathed in the sunlight in Careel Bay. (Susan Wright)

Above:
Writer Dorothea Mackellar lived here in Lovett Bay.
(Catherine Warne)

Opposite page:
Top:
Clareville, Pittwater, from West Head.
(Catherine Warne)

Bottom left:
Sprawling mangroves on Pittwater's southern end.
(Rob Jenson)

Bottom right:
Canoeing in Towlers Bay.
(Catherine Warne)

Left:
The picturesque charm of cottages at Currawong.
(Rob Jenson)

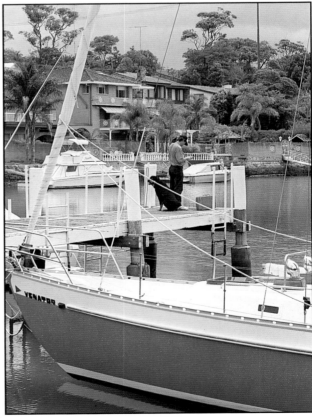

Above:
Looking from Bayview back to Royal Prince Alfred Yacht Club. (Susan Wright)

Left:
"The fish that didn't get away." Ron Webber, Simon Deathridge and Matthew Webber of Newport Arms Hotel Fishing Club. (Newport Arms Hotel)

Opposite page:
Top:
Scotland Island from Ku-Ring-Gai Chase National Park. (Catherine Warne)

Bottom left and right:
Expensive homes and pleasure craft in Yachtsmans' Paradise, Newport. (Susan Wright)

The popular Newport Arms Hotel looks across Pittwater to Bayview. (Rob Jenson)

Boats are a big part of life in Pittwater. (Rob Jenson)

was favoured by bakers because of its intense heat and because it burns to an ash. The Olivers built ships in Pittwater, one a green painted lugger, the *Thomas and Martha*. A portion of the Oliver land included Tumbledown Dick Hill and bullock drays were used to carry the cut timber and shingles to the wharf at Pittwater to be conveyed by ship to Sydney.

As a pioneering family the Oliver family would have had countless tales of Pittwater. Various sources relate that Mrs. Oliver, while telling stories to her children on a shady veranda, sat with a loaded musket within arm's reach to frighten local Aborigines after they had earlier looted a paddock of potatoes. In 1862 Oliver had a farm at Lovett's Bay and grew a variety of fruit trees and vines. By marriage the Olivers were connected to the Shaw family and their family saga is the story of the early days of Pittwater.

The district's first school was held in the small Methodist Church at Church Point and the first teacher, Samuel Morrison, was appointed on 1 May 1884. He married Emma Chave, daughter of a local orchardist in 1887. In that year his remote school house was honoured with a visit by Sir Henry Parkes, five times Premier of New South Wales and remembered as the Father of Federation.

The little graveyard close to where the church stood is a special place. It clings to the steep incline of the hillside above the roadway and Pittwater is glimpsed through the trunks of the spotted gums and soft casuarinas.

High above Church Point on a hilltop a trigonometrical station was established in 1883.

At weekends Church Point is crowded with cars. The wharf has a tiny office and a boat service is provided across to Scotland Island and

A Henry King photograph of Scotland Island when it supported orchards.

A family boil the billy above Scotland Island, n.d.

other parts of Pittwater. In 1909 a post office opened near the original wharf and the boatshed and store of James Booth were located one on either side of the wharf. Booth, an old identity, had two luggers, the *Claribel and Menina* and carried visitors on excursions and fishing trips around Pittwater.

By the late 1920s the first Pasadena stood on the site of Booth's store and was operated by C.F. Wymark. It was two storeyed with a veranda fronting the street and included a store and residence. Since that date there has been a Pasadena restaurant at Church Point operated by a variety of owners. Pasadena on Pittwater is a restaurant/motel conference centre and the view across Pittwater is unchanging and superb. The present owners have plans to redevelop the site with $1.5M improvements, including an additional level and tavern. Residents of Church Point and Scotland Island are concerned about increased noise levels and that the development will spoil the village atmosphere of Church

Point. The Church Point newsagency has closed with the redevelopment although it is hoped a new newsagency will be re-established. The shop has served the community for nearly sixty years, delivering newspapers to Scotland Island and other communities around Pittwater.

It is inevitable that change and progress will with time intrude on Church Point and Pittwater. There is still the weatherboard Church Point Post Office and store close to the wharf. A receiving office opened at Church Point on 1 January 1909 with James Booth the first receiving office keeper. The post office opened on 15 May 1912. The present post office/store has a small coffee shop with tables and umbrellas beside Pittwater and the comings and goings on the water may be observed while lunching.

Allan Corbett recorded his memories of the area in a history of Church Point and McCarrs Creek. During the 1930s he was building a house at McCarrs Creek and settled

The Church Point Wharf in 1904.

permanently there in 1947. He ran a building business and had a home-made boat to transport timber and tools to sites around the bays. Corbett died in February 1992. He wrote

'Opposite the church on a lovely sandy beach stood Church Point store and post office. This consisted of a large boatshed with an annexe out the side to store the more bulky articles such as bags of potatoes, onions, bulk kerosene, and an old phone which was a trunk line to Sydney.

'The entrance to the store from the roadside was by a very steep ramp, which in rainy weather became smeared with clay and caused you to enter far more precipitously than consistent with decorum.

The store was owned by a Mr Simpson who owned a fruit and flower orchard on the opposite side of the road known as "Simpson's Gardens". This was separated from the church property by Quartersessions Road, then only a track. The orchard must have extended pretty near to Baroona Avenue though I am not sure when this road was built. The quality of the products was superb. I don't know where he marketed the fruit, but I think he used to take the flowers to town. I have seen him board the 7.30 am "bus" (Napier or Berliet) on Monday morning with loads of blooms. He lived in a lovely little country type house about half way along his property. It was partly constructed of bush timber and was shrouded in wisteria.

'In the late teens or early 20s (presumably Corbett's later teens or

63

during his early twenties) the farm was wound up, the land subdivided and Eastview Street created. Simpson's house was later occupied by a Mr. Orford (or Alford) and for many years he and his daughter ran a morning and afternoon tea room on the front verandah. They were particularly noted for their scones. They called the place "The Green Frog" and for many years it was popular as the terminating spot for an afternoon car drive from Sydney. (Incidentally, the name of his boat was "The Croak"!)

'With the disappearance of the Simpsons, the store was taken over by one Alfie Burton, who lived on the far shore of Lovett Bay and used to commute to and from Church Point in a cumbersome old launch called the A.C.B. He also built a large weatherboard edifice with attic accommodation about 100 yards along the road from the store towards McCarrs Creek. It was built out over the water with a verandah around two sides and they set up and a morning and afternoon tea business.'[87]

Later the Church Point store was owned by Mr. Hummerston, then Mr. Becket and their respective wives and again at a later date became a boatshed/store.

After the Beckets left a Holgo Jensen and his wife were the storekeepers. Allan Corbett recalls that around 1926 the old boatshed/store was taken to the southern end of Scotland Island. The new store was erected approximately where the present Pasadena stands - built of stone with residence and garage where boats were stored. It was destroyed by fire and a new store was built in the early 1930s on the site of today's store and post office. Today's upstairs section was the original attic residence. Since that time the store has had a number of owners.

Church Point retains its relaxed, time-warped atmosphere where the pressures of the 1990s may be forgotten. Near the store the men at the Co-op, who spend much of their time on the water delivering groceries around the area, would be happy to see Pittwater kept a secret but realise tourism is sure to discover it one day.

The Scotland Island Traders Co-operative Society has its office on the Church Point ferry wharf. The co-op promises 'Fruit and vegetables, excellent meat, booze, Saturday papers, bread, croissants, fresh seafood, locally grown salad mixes, homemade pasta, organic vegetables — all ordered before 11 a.m. Thursday will be delivered TO YOUR DOOR![88]' Many suburban households who face the weekly supermarket hassle would envy the service.

In addition the co-op will handle dry cleaning, laundry, building and hardware orders, shoe repairs and bulk spring water deliveries. For an extra fee bulky items are also delivered. The co-op also has a fax facility and photocopying service.

The small ferries depart from Church Point Wharf offering a regular service to Pittwater's residents and visitors. There is a continuity to Pittwater's history and its geography ensures students still travel by boat to attend school. At Church Point the school special ferry runs at 7.30 and 7.50 am and there is a 3 pm return trip. The mail run leaves daily at 10.10 am.

The tiny wooden ferry pulls out from its wharf and heads for Scotland Island. There are local residents heading home with shopping and a few visitors. Three of the latter are German women but resident in Australia for many years. They live at Normanhurst and have enjoyed the trip previously and driven down to Church Point to spend another day on Pittwater - 'It is very beautiful'. Perhaps they are unaware that Pittwater's first white explorer, Governor Arthur Phillip also had German ancestry. His father was a teacher of languages from Frankfurt.

The ferry is low in the water and sends a white wake across the water's surface while the engine chugs steadily.

Scotland Island

Scotland Island rises like the forested summit of a mountain from the waters of Pittwater. It is a short boat's ride across from Church Point. An early photograph shows the island in its pristine beauty, tree clad and apparently uninhabited. It looks as it must have appeared when the waters of Pittwater knew only the dugout canoes of the Aborigines.

The island is closely associated with Andrew Thompson. Thompson arrived in Sydney as a convict on the transport *Pitt* with the Second Fleet in 1792. He was sentenced to fourteen years transportation for the theft of cloth, valued at about £10, from the shop of a merchant. Thompson was born c.1773 and was therefore about nineteen on his arrival in Sydney. His father was a weaver, manufacturer and dyer at Kirk Yetholm in Scotland and Andrew had been educated at a parochial school until forced to leave due to ill health. He was studying for the excise service when arrested.

In the colony Thompson was appointed to the police service in 1793 and served with distinction at Toongabbie and other areas. In 1796 Governor Hunter appointed him to the Green Hills (Windsor) and he rose to Chief Constable, a position he held until 1808. The Reverend Samuel Marsden praised Thompson's actions in the 1806 Hawkesbury floods when he saved the lives of 101 residents, plucking them from their rooftops in one of his boats.

Thompson had received an absolute pardon in 1797. He built the first toll bridge at Windsor, established a brewery and a hotel, managed Governor Bligh's Hawkesbury farms, owned ships, a tannery and salt works. In 1804 Governor King had helped Thompson set up a salt manufacturing plant in Broken Bay. The first site was Mullet Island (now Dangar Island) on the Hawkesbury River but later Thompson moved his salt works to Scotland Island, named for his homeland. In 1809 Thompson was granted by Lieutenant Governor Paterson '120 acres on island near the southern extremity of Pittwater Bay - being the first bay on the south west side of the south head of Broken Bay. Rent: 3 shillings per year commencing after 5 years.'[89] This grant was later approved by Governor Macquarie. The grant reserved to the government 'the right of making a Public Road through the island and also reserving for the use of the Crown such timber as may be deemed fit for naval purposes'.[90]

At the salt works on the island Thompson extracted salt from seawater by means of an oil burner. He was able to extract 200 lbs (90 kgs) of salt a week. A house was built and a ship slipway. It was rumoured Thompson operated an illicit still on Scotland Island.

Governor Macquarie was a valued friend and appointed him a Justice of the Peace and Chief Magistrate on the Hawkesbury. Macquarie described him as a man of 'sober habits and good character'[91] The 'exclusives' of the colony hated and maligned Thompson. Macquarie appointed him a trustee of the new turnpike road from Sydney to Parramatta which antagonised the Reverend Marsden, another appointee. Marsden retired in anger to his farms.

By 1810 Thompson was ill as a result of his strenuous efforts in the Hawkesbury floods of 1809 and he died on 22 October 1810. His estate was valued at between £20,000 and £25,000. In his will he bequeathed a quarter of his fortune to Governor Macquarie.

Macquarie wrote that Thompson's death 'affected Mrs. Macquarie and myself deeply - for we both had a most sincere and affectionate esteem for our good and most lamented departed friend'.[92]

Thompson's was the first burial in the cemetery of St Matthew's Church at Windsor and Governor Macquarie composed the long epitaph carved on his tombstone which may still be viewed today.

Before his death Andrew Thompson had laid the keel of a vessel which he named the *Geordy*. The *Sydney Gazette* of 24 November 1810 states

On Wednesday, the 14th of the present month, a launch took place at Scotland Isle, Pitt Water, of a vessel of 18 tons, said to be one of the finest of her berthen ever built in the Colony.- She makes part of the devised property of the late Mr. Thompson, who at the laying down of her keel gave her the name of the Geordy.

Following Thompson's death the island was initially rented to William Mason for £120 for three years. It was then purchased by Robert Lathrop Murray. In 1812 Scotland Island was offered for sale and the *Sydney Gazette* advertisement declared it contains 'one hundred and twenty acres of good soil, extensive salt-works, a good dwelling-house and stores, labourers' rooms, and every convenience suitable for a fishery, or shipbuilding, also a vessel of about ninety tons, partly built, still on the stocks.'[93]

In the 1920s the foundations of Thompson's house and the remnants of a wharf were still in existence.

The island was offered for sale in 1813, 1814 and again in 1815 when it was divided into thirteen lots. In the *Sydney Gazette* of 21 August 1819 Scotland Island is again on the market but was not sold. Maybanke Anderson[94] says that in 1868 a stranger appeared at Pittwater to lay claim to Scotland Island stating his father had purchased it in 1819. The Sydney Gazette advertisement of that year declares that the island is the property of R.A. Murray. The stranger claimed his name was D'Arcy Wentworth Latrobe Murray. He stated his father had been Secretary to the Duke of Kent, Queen Victoria's father. He claimed to be in possession of letters sent by the Duke to his father after the latter had come to Australia. Murray claimed he had come expressly to Australia to give the letters to Prince Alfred, the Duke of Edinburgh, then touring Australia, so they might be returned to the Queen. Murray also hoped the Prince might obtain a government appointment for him in New South Wales. The Duke of Kent died on 23 January 1820 six days before King George III and the brothers were buried at night at Windsor.

Murray was not successful in his claim. Charles Swancott[95] states a John Dickson had earlier laid claim to Scotland Island and when he died in 1843 he bequeathed it to his sons. The sons all died within a few years but James and David Dickson had given a seven year lease to Charles Jenkins and Joseph Benn who arrived at Scotland Island about 1855. They later discovered the Dicksons had no title to the island and Jenkins and Joseph Benn received a Certificate of Title as tenants in common after thirty years tenancy of the island. Jenkins died in 1892.

Joe and Mrs Benn are a legend on Scotland Island. Born in Antwerp, Belgium, Benn's name was in fact Ambrol Josef Diercknecht. He had apparently run away to sea and was soon a trader in Sydney owning a number of vessels, the *William and Betsy* and the *Lady of the Lake*. The *William and Betsy* foundered off Port Stephens and the *Lady of the Lake* was wrecked at Long Reef, near Collaroy.

Benn rebuilt Andrew Thompson's house and is said to have treasured a packet of old letters and documents but instructed they were to be burned shortly before his death.

Islands and treasure are synonymous and Scotland Island has its tale of treasure troves. The Belgian had brought Mrs. Benn to the island and she acquired the title of Queen of Scotland Island. Nell Almeida of Narrabeen, who is connected with the Benn family, says the family always used to say they were related to royalty, apparently for the Queen of Scotland Island.

Mrs Benn was a small, dark woman with gentle manners, who wore remnants of fine clothes and some beautiful jewellery. She helped the islanders in illness and also acted as midwife. J.S.N. Wheeler remembered 'seeing her once, an old lady, rowing herself across to Scotland Island in the teeth of a stiff nor'wester' around 1905.[96]

In her last years Mrs Benn grew eccentric and gave belongings to friends but a story persists that she buried the greater part of her treasure on the island.

Even earlier in Andrew Thompson's time it was claimed a three legged pot full of holey dollars was hidden by two men who came from Sydney with a boatload of stolen treasure.

Joseph Benn died on 29 March 1900. Benn called himself Joe Benn or Binn and was described in his will as Joseph Benn. Benn left an estate of £35 to his wife, Kathleen. It was only following his death that Benn's true name was revealed.

In 1900 a survey was made of Scotland Island and its area was 129 acres, 2 roods (52.5 hectares). Thompson's grant stated it covered 120 acres (48.5 hectares). Again in 1906 Surveyor Dobbie surveyed the island and land was offered for public auction on Saturday 10 November 1906.

Charles Swancott in his book *Dee Why to Barrenjoey and Pittwater* states that in 1911 it was proposed a Naval College should be established on Scotland Island giving the *Sun* newspaper of 29 September 1911 as his reference. Although a very frail copy of this paper has been checked at the Mitchell Library, State Library of New South Wales, no reference to the college was found.

During the 1920s a Mr. Fitzpatrick began to develop the island. There were few houses although Yamba stood on the western side of the island and Bangalla on the south-eastern side. Both houses still survive.

Scotland Island is encircled by houses nestled amongst the tall gums and vegetation. The water is very shallow close inshore. There are boatsheds, jetties, stone walls, yachts and boats and a number of wharves where the ferries call in if anyone wishes to disembark or passengers are waiting on the wharf. The ferry's skipper Colin is English born and a Pittwater resident who for relaxation sails his yacht here on Pittwater or down the coast to Sydney Harbour. The harbour is 'a bit of a rat race nowadays' but Pittwater is placid and there is enough work available. The locals know the skippers well and Lennie Duck is a Pittwater identity. The original ferry service was commenced about forty five years ago by Keith Egan and Lennie Duck has been associated with the service for the last thirty years. Originally from Mosman, Duck had a milk run, but married a Clareville girl and started work with the Church Point ferry. He knows all the locals, helps to transport their children back and forth to school and declares that the residents of Pittwater are 'a special brand of people.' Nowadays Duck also caretakes a property at Lovett Bay and declares this is probably his 'favourite spot'. There is fresh air everywhere and he foresees no great changes to Pittwater. After all the mainland to Palm Beach already has its houses and the national park area behind the West Pittwater settlements limits development.

At the Tennis Wharf is Andrew Thompson Park and in the late

1950s Percy Gledhill and the Manly Warringah and Pittwater Historical Society unveiled a monument here to Andrew Thompson. The party came over from Church Point in the ferry to Tennis Wharf, Mr. Gledhill as always in his three piece suit and felt hat. He loved these occasions and usually arranged a camera crew to record the event to be shown on a Cinesound newsreel.

From Andrew Thompson Park a road winds around the island. The foreshore area measures roughly 2-2.5 kilometres and walking at a brisk pace it would take approximately 35 minutes to walk the distance. The island covers forty two hectares and island roads are untarred; locals use four-wheeled drive vehicles. Several streets plunge up the steep sides of the island to the summit and Elizabeth Park. The island rises 100 metres above sea level. It is a strenuous walk, heavily forested and the magpies chortle among the trees. The roads tend to list due to the run off in heavy rains and erosion is a problem.

Scotland Island has a population of 550 although Residents Association stalwart Lester Warburton declares the islanders are a fertile lot and the local kindy is bursting at the seams. The island has 365 blocks, 280 houses and permanent and weekender residents. About 60% are permanent. Many are young families. In the days of the 'hippies' some came to the island attracted by cheap rents. Now the water police provide a service and, if necessary, can convey a patient to Mona Vale Hospital in fifteen to twenty minutes, probably quicker than some suburban areas.

While life on an island may seem idyllic there are disadvantages and lack of water is sometimes a problem. In 1967 Scotland Island residents voted against a Government assisted water supply scheme. A special levy would have been applied in addition to council rates and the Water Board's charges for supplies. A long dry spell or a drought can cause problems.

Once the island relied on kerosene lighting but in 1965 'the lights were turned on'.[97]

The islanders gathered to celebrate the occasion with drinks and a plate supper. All had left the new light switches turned on and when an official pulled the switch at 10 p.m. the island 'lit up like Christmas.'[98]

Lester Warburton, who for the past twenty two years has been Editor of the local newspaper, the Scotland Island News, came from Curl Curl to settle on the island. He claims 90% of people ask 'Where is Scotland Island?' Initially he enlightened inquirers but then grew canny and decided to keep the island a secret. This is very much a Pittwater attitude. Both the Scotland Island Residents Association and the Coasters Retreat Association shun the word 'progress' in their titles. 'That's the last thing they wanted'.[99]

On an island bushfire could be a disaster and despite its rejection of too much progress the islanders are not foolhardy. At the Tennis Wharf the local fire brigade has its headquarters and has recently acquired a new shed for its equipment. Hopefully it will never be used for a serious conflagration.

One suggestion many of the islanders have strongly opposed is a vehicular punt service to the island. A punt and cars would end its peaceful isolation and inevitably bring more visitors, tarred roads and the sprawl of suburbanism.

Not that the islanders are staid and unfriendly. In their community hall they have musical shows and operate a theatre restaurant. The Scotland Island Players first show for 1992 was a humorous play, 'Bedroom Farce.' Once a month a jazz and rock evening is held which shakes up the ghosts of Scotland Island.

There is also the annual Scotland Island Fair and visitors may take the ferry across the water to enjoy the fair. There are arts and crafts, a sausage sizzle, live music, a children's show, a cross country race, stalls of 'kids' clothing' and pottery. There are also demonstrations of Tai Chi, a Water Police demonstration, a Flare demonstration, fire extinguishers, Identikid photos, Maritime Services Board boat licensing, tarot card readings and a cafe offering morning tea and lunch.

One rather notorious association with the island was the famous Madam, Tilly Devine (1900-1970). Tilly was born Matilda Mary Twiss in London and during World War I married an Australian soldier, James Devine. In 1919 Devine returned to Sydney and his wife followed the next year in a war-bride ship, the *Waimana*. In Sydney Tilly worked as a prostitute with her husband as protector. From 1921-1925 she had 79 convictions for offences relating to prostitution and the couple became more involved in underworld activities including the sly-grog traffic. By World War II she was 'Queen of the 'Loo' and a rival of the other infamous madam, Kate Leigh. Tilly divorced Devine in 1943 and in 1945 married a seaman named Parsons. In 1953 she sailed to England to see the Coronation of Queen Elizabeth II.

Tilly Devine had a hideaway on Scotland Island. She would often arrive on a Friday night at Church Point with her body guards to be ferried across to the island. She was said to have given her working girls a restful holiday on Scotland Island and also to have hidden a cache of ill-gotten tax-free gains some time in the 1930s.

Lester Warburton says he was diving on one occasion when he sighted an old steel box. No doubt his heart skipped a beat being fully aware of the stories of hidden wealth. He came ashore to get equipment while a neighbour excitedly shouted 'That's the treasure'. Eventually the 'find' was hauled up. Instead of holey dollars or Tilly Devine's illegal fortune up came an old Silent Knight refrigerator!

McCarrs Creek

Just past Church Point McCarrs Creek enters Pittwater. The roadway follows the foreshore to Browns Bay and climbs to Ku-ring-gai Chase. Not far from Church Point an obelisk was erected by the Manly Warringah and Pittwater Historical Society in 1943 recalling the early surveys of the creek by Captain John Hunter in 1789 and W.R. Govett in 1829. Govett was moved to comment 'Pittwater received a romantic creek'.[100] Captain Sidney during his survey in 1868 called the creek Pitt Inlet.

The creek originates near Tumbledown Dick Hill. (Sydney journalist and later editor, David McNicol, caused a furore in the 1950s when he wanted this distinctly named hill renamed for South American patriot, General San Martin.)

In the heat haze of summer the water of McCarrs Creek sparkles through the trees and home dwellers have discovered an idyllic hideaway.

The road from Church Point was originally Quarter Sessions Road, then Browns Road when it reached Browns Bay and McCarrs Creek Road when continued to Terrey Hills.

In the early 1920s the road went only to a local house called Rostrevor, owned by the Ireland family. There were few families in the area and Browns Bay was named for George Brown who owned forty-one acres called Waterview granted to him on 30 June 1880. The bay was named at the request of the Manly Warringah and Pittwater Historical Society. The house was destroyed by a fire around 1913. The other early residence, Sunnyside, survives on the hill among more modern homes.

The road climbs steeply from the water and in the early years when it was rough it was not unusual for a sulky or an early model car to slip over the bank. An old photograph shows the natural bush and beach area described as 'Ireland's Beach, Pittwater, via Manly, N.S.W.'

The early settlers lived isolated lives, they grew vegetables and planted fruit trees. This is casuarina country and the road still passes through the forest. Called she-oaks by English settlers in Sydney because of a similarity in the grain of the wood to English oak the trees were early used for shingles, axe handles and yokes. On Pittwater the casuarina timber was transported by vessel to Sydney to be burnt in baker's ovens and used for the shingles. A mass of stone in the area was locally called the ballast heap and claimed to have been carried as ballast by the ships on the return voyage to Pittwater.

Land around McCarrs Creek and Browns Bay was subdivided at the turn of the century. One area was called 'By the Lake Estate' but the first house was not built until 1916. The only access to Church Point was by boat or following cow tracks over the hills.

The bush clad hills attracted timber getters and in the 1920-1930s a team of timber cutters worked up the hills beside McCarrs Creek. The timber was tied to a skiff and rowed to the area near Ireland's house and then transferred to a truck. Much of the timber became telegraph poles between Mona Vale and Palm Beach.

The roadside has a variety of vegetation - cabbage tree palms engulfed by convolvulus, the blue morning glory.

Under the casuarina forest the steep incline of the hillside is carpeted with fresh green bracken. McCarrs Creek Reserve was once mangrove flat and a small area of mangroves survives. Here are young planted casuarinas and the reserve is sheltered by the shadowed hills. Boats are upturned and tied to wooden posts and a vessel, flying a faded stars and stripes flag, is anchored by the mangroves.

Between 1959 and 1973 McCarrs Creek was assaulted by a sand dredge company. Permission had been granted by the New South Wales Department of Lands to allow dredging of Browns Bay to a depth of 12 feet. Residents endured the noise pollution while the creek was dredged, mud, shell, charcoal and sand were separated and the once clear waters befouled by oil and dieseline spillage waste. The work eventually gave creek access for boats up to 16 metres.

A favourite area on the creek was always the Silent Pool, a secluded area fed by Lower Gledhill Falls. Natural bushland, reflective waters and sandstone rocks create a magic spot.

The names hereabouts speak of a more leisured era: Crystal Creek, Cicada Glen, Crystal Creek and Cascades. The names were officially bestowed c.1945 but were in common use earlier. Cicada Glen Creek was once Bumpo Creek, said to be so called as at high tide boats were bumped from one side of the creek to the other by snags and mangroves.

'The Duckhole' is within Ku-ring-gai Chase National Park on McCarrs Creek. It is said that in the 1890s the area was the haunt of ducks. The sun baked sandstone rocks create rock pools one to two metres deep and the area is sheltered by bushland. At weekends it is a popular picnic area but when deserted the spirits of the vanished Aboriginal people reclaim their land.

Approximately 400 metres upstream are located Upper Gledhill Falls. Both the Upper and Lower Gledhill Falls were named in honour of Percy W. Gledhill. Gledhill came to Manly in 1913 'filled with the desire - in view of my grandfather having been the first chemist in Manly and district - to put together what information I could gather on the early days of "The Village".'[101] In 1924 he achieved his aim of creating a local historical society.

The name McCarrs Creek is used on the survey of J. Larmer in 1832 and appears to have been first officially used in 1835 in a proclamation of the Parishes of the County of Cumberland. As a portion of the creek is within the National Park area there are still wildflowers along its banks, although perhaps not in as great profusion as in the 1930s when over 90 species were identified.

From the Duck Hole the road sweeps around towards Akuna Bay and West Head within the magnificent Ku-ring-gai Chase National Park (see page 85).

The National Park area borders the western shore of Pittwater and there are numerous settlements hugging the shoreline. From McCarrs Creek and facing towards Scotland Island are Elvina and Lovett Bays.

Elvina Bay

In 1842 pioneer William Oliver was granted 30 acres (12 hectares) of land at Elvina Bay. During a visit to the area, Oliver discovered a forest of red oak and was soon exploiting the timber. The forest rang to the sound of axes and the trees, mostly 15 metres tall and 45 centimetres in diameter, were dragged by horse from the forest and cut into billets. The timber was shipped to Sydney in vessels built by the Olivers and Shaws.

The Oliver connection still survives on Pittwater for Holley Marine Services is operated by R. and M. Oliver. They own a timber tug, barge and crane - the *Bringa*. Painted in the original green and gold colours of its heyday the *Bringa* is some 82 years old and still working. The *Bringa* was built in 1910 of oregon, with a tallow wood deck and copper-sheathed hull.

Elvina Bay is the first settlement north from McCarrs Creek. These settlements on this western shore of Pittwater have a similarity to remote fishing villages found in the outflung regions of Scotland. They are backed by the magnificence of Ku-ring-gai Chase and there are walking tracks within the park to the various bays.

The 1886 Parish Map shows Oliver's land between Elvina Bay and Lovett Bay, 50 acres (20 hectares) to A.H. McCulloch, Jnr., at the head of the bay and 40 acres (16 hectares) to F. Fahl on the southern shore. Andrew Hardie McCulloch, Jnr., purchased his land in 1862 for £50. The bay itself is unnamed on the map.

Even on a winter's day Pittwater is magnificent. There might be an icy steel to the colour of the water, the sky is a washed out blue with wisps of covering cloud, the shadows of the hills are deeper and the breeze brisker but it retains the calm and serenity of a summer's day.

At the mouth of McCarrs Creek there is a jumble of moored vessels and the local Church Point ferry, *Curlew* chugs across to Scotland Island. The only sound are the steady rhythm of the ferry's engine and the calls of the birds from the forested hills of the island. The ferry turns from the island for Hall's Wharf on Pittwater's western shore, thence into Lovett Bay and Elvina Bay. The foreshore areas are speckled with houses, jetties and boatsheds. Shags sit on wooden piers, gulls soar overhead and an ochre sailed schooner of the Scotland Island Sailing Club glides quietly by.

The sun slants down the trunks of the gums and strikes the boatsheds bordering Elvina Bay. The water is cut by the ferry's bow and is shadowed with a luminosity like a Monet painting. The houses blend with the landscape and at the head of the bay is a mud flat and autumn toned trees glowing amongst the small settlement. The view from the bay is across to the western shore of Scotland Island and there is a foreshore park area. It looks a wonderful spot for children - so much to explore and discover and no busy highways with deafening traffic to tear at nerves and threaten life and limb.

Beashels Yacht Basin Pty. Ltd. is a prominent landmark of Elvina Bay. The building is of sun bleached timber and yachts and boats are on the slips. The name Beashel is a famous one in yachting circles and in May 1992 Pittwater yachtsman Colin Beashel finished equal first in the Star keelboat class but lost the Gold Medal on a countback at the Spa Olympic classes regatta in Holland. Colin Beashel was a member of the sailing team for the 1992 Barcelona Olympics. The ferry stops at two wharves in the bay, Elvina Bay North and Elvina Bay. Locals climb aboard, exchange news and local gossip and are friendlier than the passengers on a suburban bus lost in their own thoughts and worries.

To the north between Elvina Bay and Lovett Bay is Rocky Point. It is bush clad and a few mangroves survive on the foreshore rocks. On the point is Trincomalee, a wooden home with a Norfolk Pine shadowing the roof. This was the home of the Neilsen family. Juanita Neilsen who published a local Kings Cross newspaper and who disappeared in the 1970s at the time of the fight to save Victoria Street, Kings Cross was a family member. This area was part of William Oliver's land. The Olivers erected a dwelling in 1862 and the family lived on the estate for some time. J.S.N. Wheeler[102] recalls that earlier the point was Flood's Peninsula (a man named Flood built the first cottage on the estate in 1890). In 1891 a J. Booth built a timber residence here called the Red House for an artist and music teacher, Signor Stefani. Stefani had an Italian wife and Wheeler muses that this part of Pittwater may have reminded the couple of the Italian Lakes. However Stefani, it appears was an Englishman, with the more prosaic name of Arthur Stephens, although Wheeler claims he was 'an aristocratic Englishman'.[103]

The house was later renamed Wyandra and it had baths, wharf, boatshed and tennis court. An Italian style balustrade flanked stone steps which led to a grassy bank in front of the house.

Also in this area was Ventnor - a brick and timber squat cottage with low verandas. It was owned by the Crawford Brothers who had a brickworks here. Only a few remnants of the house remained in 1967. In the 1880s near the north entrance to Lovett Bay Frederick Chave had the finest orchard in the district growing figs, lemons, oranges and olives. There was also a perfect vine where J.S.N. Wheeler bought a bucketful of grapes for one shilling. He claimed the vine grew in a dingle halfway between Chave's house and the road. Chave, who died in 1898, was buried at Church Point.

Elvina Bay may also be reached via a bush walk from West Head Road within Ku-ring-gai Chase National Park. In spring wildflowers may be admired along the 2.5 km track, which has some steep grades. There are Aboriginal rock carvings of the people who once roamed this area along the route of the track.

Lovett Bay

Around Rocky Point is Lovett Bay which Captain F.W. Sidney named in his 1868-1872 survey Night Bay.

Surrounded by high hills Flagstaff Lookout gives extensive views over Pittwater and Broken Bay. .

The bay is named for Pittwater settler John Lovett who resided in the area from 1836. The name Lovett for the bay was first used in 1862 when George Commins surveyed 40 acres (16 hectares) of shoreline land. For the settlers it was a long route to Sydney for they chose to drive from this part of Pittwater by horse-drawn vehicle or on horseback to Quaker's Hat and Folly Point in Middle Harbour and on to Blues Point to cross to Sydney.

One of the features of Lovett Bay is a huge outcrop of sheer rock where a waterfall cascades 30 metres down the hillside in rainy weather. Governor Phillip noted three such waterfalls at Pittwater during his visit in 1788. The falls, Linda Falls, provided a water supply for early homes with water carried from a pool at the top of the falls by an iron pipe down the cliff and thence to the peninsula's highest point to fill a concrete reservoir. The water service dated from 1891 when a later resident of the old Oliver property, a Mr. Williams, subdivided the land as the Ventnor Estate.

Alan Corbett[104] recalls the old picnic site when the area was Ku-ring-gai Chase Trust. Located at the head of Lovett Bay from 'a public wharf on the northern shore a path about four feet wide (1.2 metres) led alongside the shallow tidal waters'[105] to the picnic area, where there were facilities for 'boiling the billy'. Corbett says there were masses of wildflowers and 'a series of unique caves'[106] and the path which led to Flagstaff. At weekends the paths were busy with crowds of picnickers.

Lovett Bay is a beautiful bay sheltered by the towering hillsides. The local ferry glides gently to the steps of the little wharf and it is suddenly a different world. A boat lies on a tiny fragment of beach and there are stone signs proclaiming 'Lovett Bay' and '1895'. On the rock face behind the segment of beach is a carved Aborigine face, half veiled by a casuarina. Apparently in 1895 a local council worker building the stone foreshore area let fancy take flight with something a little more creative and carved the face and made the two stone signs.

Ahead is a sign 'Tarrangaua' and stone steps and stone paved driveway lead up the hillside to this fine house. The waters of the bay are placid viewed between the gums, native violets peep from the grass and suddenly there is Tarrangaua. The house, designed by Hardy Wilson in 1924, has stone foundations and its walls are cream painted brick, strong columns front the veranda and the view is the bay. This house was the retreat of writer Dorothea Mackellar (1885-1968) author of Australia's best known poem 'My Country'. Journalist Di Morrissey recalls Dorothea Mackellar in *"Warringah 1988"*[107] as 'a rarely glimpsed figure in black who smiled at you vaguely.' In Australia's Bicentennial year 1988 Dorothea Mackellar was the subject of a chamber opera commissioned by Warringah Shire Council. Composed by Alan Holley with libretto by Jyoti Brunsdon the opera includes the words

Dear Lovett Bay - so quiet and far from
(Surprised) - just about everything!
The friendly rocks, the cool
embrace of water.[108]

Behind the house a path twists around Lovett Bay. It is almost Dorothea Mackellar's world 'Green tangle of the brushes; Where lithe lianas coil, And orchids deck the tree-tops, And ferns the warm dark soil.'.[109] There are tall straight eucalypts, cabbage tree palms, fronds of soft maiden hair fern, bright green moss covered rocks, half hidden fungi and the sun striking the clumps of bracken beside the path. There are staggering glimpses of the bay and the distant rock cluttered cliffs. A lone kookaburra laughs raucously in the bush.

The famous 'Chips' Rafferty and his wife were earlier residents of Lovett Bay. They had a holiday house here as an escape from Chips' busy career as actor and movie star. Pittwater has been a refuge for many, including writer George Farwell, who one day set off for the city with his children to visit his publisher. He arrived back at Pittwater minus the children, simply having forgotten them.

On the shore of Lovett Bay boats are upended near the wharf and workmen are busy working on a vessel on the slips of the boatshed. The vessel is named *Kintyre* and again there is the imagery of distant Scottish isles. But the sun is bright and the sound of hammering breaks the silence. There are fallen logs near the path and the verdant lushness of undergrowth. In the bay are a few mangroves and the cliffs hide the second waterfall which lies at the head of the bay. Here, too, a creek enters Lovett Bay once called Salvation Creek but in 1939 renamed Larmers Creek for the surveyor.

In 1895 four men were employed at the bay constructing tracks to The Lookout, the Flat Rock and the waterfall. They also built a causeway and jetty. Even earlier, in the 1880s, Joe Carrio, the son-in-law of pioneer William Oliver had 40 acres (16 hectares) of land near the causeway. He owned a ketch called *The Maid of Australia* and ran it to Sydney carrying firewood and staghorns and tree-ferns torn from the bush and sold in the city.

A new track was built in 1917 to Coal and Candle Creek and near the lookout was the tunnel, made by the weathering of the sandstone.

A small stream of water tumbles over Linda Falls but in a deluge the falls are magnificent, cascading to the bay. Near the track to these falls on the southern side of Lovett Bay is the lonely grave of Frederick Oliver, son of William, who died in 1867.

At the small wharf there is a grey haired neatly bearded man who takes the orange flag from its post to signal the ferry captain to call at the wharf. He once lived at Wahroonga and at Neutral Bay and enjoyed sailing on Sydney Harbour but for over a decade has made his home at Lovett Bay. Every Australian carries his art work in wallet or handbag for he is Gordon Andrews, who designed our original decimal currency. He shares the Pittwater philosophy of wishing to keep the area a secret but chats amiably as the ferry heads back to Church Point. In 1992 the new five dollar note was introduced to our currency, scrapping Andrews' original design featuring Caroline Chisholm. This caused a small protest from some members of society including the Prime Minister, Paul Keating. Andrews is philosophical about the changes to the currency and says he understands the reasons behind the change. When the currency was first issued it was fun for a few months to walk into a shop and see people using 'my money' he says. The ferry arrives at Church Point and the few passengers vanish to attend to their business.

Suburban bound Sydneysiders might wonder at those who seclude themselves in these remote bays and live with discomfort such as water shortages. The bay-siders however, have found serenity where even on the first official day of winter there is blue sky, sunshine, birds singing in the bush and all appears right with the world. Small wonder that a local T shirt declares, 'Lovett Bay Somewhere on the Australian Coast'.

Youth Hostel, Hall's Wharf, Lovett Bay

Winter sunshine glows on the wattle and white cockatoos screech overhead as the ferry leaves Church Point to head across Pittwater on the 10.10 mail run. There is a brisk, fresh westerly with a clear winter sun, blue sky and shining water. The ferry is low on the water and sends ripples towards moored yachts named *Hydra* and *Portofino* recalling distant waters.

Horst, the German skipper from Hanover, smartly brings the ferry into Hall's Wharf where there is a sign informing visitors the youth hostel is open to members and is located at the end of a well signposted ten minute uphill walk. Up the steps from the wharf there are clumps of maidenhair fern and a short tunnel of young bamboos which leads to an area of open forest with tall spotted gums. There is a cacophony of bird calls and, on the uphill walk, glimpses of the waters of Pittwater.

The youth hostel is sited in a superb location looking towards Towlers Bay. The foreshore homes lose the sun early in the day but here, well up the hillside, the sun is warm and strong at midday on a winter's day.

The hostel, standing in approximately two acres of land, was once a private home. It is a single storey building with stone base and asbestos cement and stained batten wall linings with an iron roof. The hillside is terraced with stone walls. Built in 1915, the building has a heritage listing for its architectural value and in its function as a youth hostel it demonstrates a philosophy of special recreational features for young people.

The house was given to the Youth Hostel movement in 1966 by the owner and resident Ibena Isles. Interested in bushwalking and conservation before it became a popular activity Ibena Isles was a lady 'ahead of her time' according to Robert Richards who is in charge of the hostel this morning in the absence of manager, Phil Charles. A local resident, originally from Collaroy, Robert finds Pittwater is still an unspoilt area where little has changed.

The hostel accommodates 32 people and approximately 50-60 percent of visitors are from overseas, mostly from Britain. The hostel also attracts regular hostellers who love the area and return again and again. There are canoe facilities and enthusiasts may go sailing with the Scotland Island Sailing School. Surrounded by Ku-ring-gai Chase National Park the Youth Hostel enjoys the many bush walks and activities available in this area. A group of young people enthusiastically play badminton while others relax in the sunshine, enjoying the view of Towlers Bay and the laughter of the kookaburras.

Behind the hostel is a long low house blending with the hostel and environment and this too was built by Ibena Isles after she gave her home to the Youth Hostel movement. Ibena Isles retired to the Blue Mountains and has been active with the Mt. Victoria Historical Society.

On the way back down the hillside the wind moves through the tree tops of the forest. Rainbow lorikeets chatter and flit among the branches and a flock of grey and pink galahs suddenly take flight and wheel towards Pittwater. Currawongs poke around the gardens of the foreshore homes and clumps of banana palms mingle with native vegetation.

From Hall's Wharf the view is to Church Point where the houses climb the hillside behind the distant shore. The only sound is the lapping of the water, the distant drone of a motor boat and the distinctive cry of a black crow.

Towlers Bay

From Hall's Wharf the foreshore leads to Woody Point. Once Wood Point it is said to have been named for settler, Arthur Wood. Behind the point the area is called Morning Bay. Captain Sidney in his survey had named the bay Morning Bay. With common usage it became Towlers Bay for Bill Toler who had a camp in the area.

In 1886 40 acres (16 hectares) here had been granted to J.A. Blackman and in 1889 40 acres (16 hectares) to Arthur Wood.

From Hall's Wharf there is access to the Towler Track within Ku-ring-gai Chase National Park and the shales here support a forest of spotted gums (*Eucalyptus maculata*) with their distinctive mottled trunks. There are also Burrawang. Fossils of this species have been found in 200 million year old rocks. This is Hawkesbury sandstone country and the sandstone formed during the Triassic period when dinosaurs were beginning to dominate the globe.

Those who choose to live at Towlers Bay do so simply because they love it. Much of the bay is surrounded by the National Park area and from West Head Road the Bairne Tracks is an easy four kilo-metre walk to Towlers Bay. The focal point of the walk is the look-out above Towlers Bay with indescribable views over Pittwater. There are Aboriginal rock carvings on the walk and low shrubs growing on the sandstone soils - hakea, grevillea, tea tree, banksia and the scribbly gums.

At weekends Pittwater is busy but during the week it is returned to the residents who pursue their daily activities. Of course Pittwater has changed with the passage of years. Once a government powder hulk vessel carrying explosives anchored in Towlers Bay and the crew lived ashore in neat cottages. Old timers declare the fish are fewer in number and marinas now sprinkle parts of Pittwater.

A creek feeds into the headwaters of Towlers Bay and on the creek is Larmers Falls named for the surveyor who surveyed Pittwater in 1832.

Further north from Towlers Bay is Long Nose Point and Soldiers Point, the latter granted to John Andrews in 1842. Andrews had been a sergeant in Britain but later settled in Australia and received his land at Pittwater.

Coasters Retreat and Bonnie Doon

On the headland between Towlers Bay and Coasters Retreat the waters of Pittwater lap Portuguese Beach. It was at this beach that the Gonsalves family camped when fishing up the coast from Sydney. From the beach the headland sweeps around to Coasters Retreat and the Basin.

Coasters Retreat is the outer portion of the Basin. It is a yachtsman's paradise and an ideal area for picnics and relaxation but it was an area of Sydney known early to the first white settlers. The earliest use of the name for the Basin is unknown. Jim Macken suggests[110] the Basin may have been so called at the time of the survey of 1789 by Captain Hunter. Macken[111] states 'The soundings of the Basin were recorded in the diary of Lieutenant Henry Waterhouse of the First Fleet'. The name was certainly well established prior to 1835 as the area is so referred to in a grant to Robert McIntosh dated 8 April that year. Like other parts of Pittwater the early settlers acquired land around Coasters Retreat and the Basin.

McIntosh held 50 acres (20 hectares) as did John Andrews and J. McCawley. At the time of the 1828 Census McIntosh was forty six years of age and had arrived in the colony as a free settler on the *Windham* in 1814. McCawley had been a Chief Constable at Cassilis, New South Wales, and even earlier a private in the 28th Regiment before acquiring his land at Pittwater. However McIntosh and McCawley soon disposed of their grants. Pittwater provided employment for the timber getters and shell gatherers.

Coasters Retreat gave shelter to coastal vessels battling heavy weather and a refuge for the vessels caught in southerly gales. No doubt master and crew were relieved to find such shelter as Broken Bay can itself be a wild area with a heavy swell sweeping towards the Hawkesbury River. The early 1800s enumerate various vessels victim to the wild seas and environment, ships owned by well known colonial men such as Captain Thomas Reiby and Captain J. Grono of the Hawkesbury. With the loss of these vessels Hawkesbury grain and other much needed supplies were lost with the wrecks.

Coasters Retreat and the Basin are a Pittwater paradise. Blue sky and sea and brilliant sunshine provide a holiday atmosphere where holiday makers swim, sail, relax, picnic, bush walk and make the most of their leisure time. The bay leads to an inner portion, the Basin. Its dedication as a public reserve dates back to 1879. The entrance to the Basin is a narrow channel lined by towering 152 metre bush thick hills.

The local ferry from Palm Beach carries visitors across to Coasters Retreat and the Basin. There are one day visitors and holiday makers plus their luggage, clothing, holiday gear, fishing equipment, food hampers and provisions. The diesel ferry *Myra* chugs across Pittwater to Bennett's Wharf at Coasters Retreat. Since 1977 the ferry service has been operated by Peter Verrills.

A crowded Pittwater ferry in the 1920s.

Palm Beach ferry wharf on Pittwater c.1930s.

The old names keep cropping up around Pittwater. The Verrills family are of Welsh/French extraction - Verrills is a Welsh name - and the family were settled around Neutral Bay and Mosman before Albert Verrills came to Palm Beach in 1923. Albert and his family built many of the houses in the Palm Beach area, including that now owned by media mogul Kerry Packer. By marriage they are connected to the Gonsalves family and all maintain a keen interest in the family history and a great love for Pittwater.

Palm Beach Ferries is the longest established ferry service on Pittwater and at one time was owned by the Port Jackson and Manly Steamship Company, operators of the famous 'Seven Mile Ships', the Manly ferries until they were taken over by Brambles in 1972. Brambles sold off the subsidiaries and the Palm Beach service passed into private hands. In summer the demand requires a half hourly service and the round trip calls at Coasters Retreat, Bonnie Doon, the Basin, Currawong and Mackeral Beach. The ferry service also offers a sixty kilometre scenic Hawkesbury River Cruise.

As it is school holiday time the 11 am ferry from Palm Beach is busy. A group of young people with rucksacks board the ferry; there are family groups and numerous children. Waiting for the ferry to depart they consume chips, ice creams and toss bags of lollies to each other. As a race Australians are not usually given to shows of patriotism, but the young people surprisingly start singing Advance Australia Fair as the ferry pulls out from the wharf to cross the expanse of Pittwater.

On the *Myra* there are a number of interesting old photographs with captions written by Fred Verrills in 1986. One shows cattle on the land now Palm Beach Golf Course and explains the cattle belonged to Mrs. Gonsalves and George Hitchcock who had a dairy nearby. Hitchcock's house was near the beach and during a fierce storm in 1930 his house and boatshed were washed away. Hitchcock was a councillor and one time President of Warringah Shire Council. Verrills states he used to drive his horse, Nelly and a 'fine rubber tired sulky' to council meetings. He further muses Hitchcock must have been hated by council workers as he used to visit twice a day all the council works in 'A' riding. Hitchcock Park beside Careel Bay is named for the former Shire President. Fred Verrills must have enjoyed a happy childhood around Pittwater as he recalls playing on the rocks between the old Palm Beach jetty and Waratah Street. He and his mates gathered periwinkles and cooked them in salt water in an old jam tin and then pulled the flesh out with a piece of wire. He writes 'I suppose young Aboriginal children did the same before we messed it up.'[112]

Across Pittwater there are views of Lion Island, Broken Bay and northwards. Houses fringe the beach at distant Mackerel Beach and in shadow the hillsides appear deep green with almost black shadows reaching to stretches of ochre coloured sand. The ferry continues past rugged sandstone outcrops where the sun hits overhangs of orange rock. To the south up Pittwater the shore is lined with the distant masts of yachts. As the *Myra* comes to Bennett's Wharf there are clumps of seaweed beneath the surface of the water and passengers step across to the wharf and head up the pathways. Coasters Retreat is a sunny secluded retreat not accessible by road although there is a fire trail high above the houses. The path meanders past the houses following the shoreline. Land at Coasters Retreat was held by John Andrews in 1842

(although he sold his 50 acres (20 hectares) to a farmer, John Smith in 1859 for £150) and James McCawley, the ex private of the 28th Regiment and Cassilis constable.

The houses face towards Pittwater and the path is fringed with casuarinas and banksias, sandstone rocks, beaches and boats. The houses are bathed in sunshine, birds sounds fill the bush and there are stunning views back to Barrenjoey.

The Gunyah stands above the path. Correctly it is Negunya, the first house built at Coasters Retreat following the first subdivision of the land in 1921. Earlier a fisherman named Griffiths had a cabin on a subdivision near the Russell land. Negunya was erected by Percy Norton Russell. At that time, in the twenties, the area was remote although in 1881 Frederick James Jackson had arrived at the Basin. Jackson was a wealthy Sydney insurance broker and early member of the Royal Prince Alfred Yacht Club. He purchased McIntosh's Basin grant and built a seven roomed weatherboard cottage named Beechwood. Audrey Shepherd, daughter of Percy Russell, has written *The Halcyon Days of Summer on Pittwater* covering the history of Coasters Retreat from 1842 to 1992. The name Negunya is for the Aboriginal name gunya (a shelter of bark) with the letters NE placed in front for Russell's wife, Nancy Evelyn. She includes many interesting old photographs in the book including ones of the family camp sited in front of where Negunya stands and used before the house was built. Negunya is a fibro and weatherboard cottage described in a 1947 Certificate of Valuation as having four rooms, kitchen, offices, tile roof and jetty. Shepherd finds this idyllic area of Pittwater never changes and both Coasters Retreat and the Basin remain as they were in the nineteenth century. The hills are green and wooded, the well trodden bush track winds by the foreshore in front of the cottages. In earlier years the shell diggers and fisher folk frequented these same shores.

Every reference to Coasters Retreat and the Basin mentions 'Peggy' or 'Sally'. This Pittwater identity lived in a tiny house on the shore of the Basin. The yachting fraternity called her Sally and little is known of her early life. She had apparently been married to a man named Morris. Audrey Shepherd,[113] despite research into Sally's past was unable to ascertain her early history, apart from the fact that she was Mary Anne Morris. She was known to have cared for wards of the State but it was her friendship for Pittwater's yachtsmen that made her a Pittwater identity. She had a tiny two roomed stone floored cottage, the walls papered with newspaper cuttings of yachts. Sally became caretaker of Beechwood, owned by F.J. Jackson and a friend to his visiting yachtsmen. She provided the yachtsmen with coffee, hot food, eggs and milk and was given in return beer and whisky. Sally kept some cows and a jersey bull, the latter causing some trouble to the locals.

An old photograph shows Sally outside her rough hut. Probably once a fine and even comely young woman she wears a battered hat, patterned long sleeved blouse, skirt and voluminous apron. There is a reference to Sally in *Great Mackarel Beach, Ku-ring-gai Chase, Pittwater.*[114]

'Mrs. Morris owns to 80 years, and is still hale and active. In her youth she lived at Parramatta. She knew "The Flying Pieman," and well remembers the day when Lady Fitzroy was thrown out of the vice-regal carriage at Parramatta and killed.'

The Flying Pieman was the nickname of William Francis King (1807-1874) who was a Sydney character famous for his walking feats. He twice beat the coach from Windsor to Sydney, a distance of 35 miles (56 kms.), by several minutes. He always wore a top hat with coloured streamers and carried a staff also bedecked with streamers. Lady FitzRoy, the Governor's wife, was killed on 7 December 1847.

Sally died in her 84th year on 6 June 1921, which makes her birth year 1837, and was buried in Manly Cemetery. In 1922 the Pittwater yachtsmen erected a memorial sundial "In Memory of Mrs Morris (Sally)" at the Basin.

It is a beautiful walk along the foreshore path of Coasters Retreat to Bonnie Doon. The houses face the pathway while some are sheltered up the hillside. There are clumps of buttercups and the creeper, Thunbergia, or black-eyed-Susan vine, its bright orange black throated flowers tangled among the trees, a clump of red crucifix orchid, splashes of wattle and near the water tank of one house an orange tree laden with fruit. The views are to the Basin and the calls of children from its sandy beach drift across the water.

Bonnie Doon is within Ku-ring-gai Chase National Park and is a peaceful spot. The ferry calls into the wharf, called locally 'The Stone Wharf' or the 'Old Careening Wharf' and it has stood for a considerable time, having been there even in 1872. A small beach exists either side of the wharf and there are sandstone outcrops and fallen trees bleached white by the elements. A gully leads up into thick bush and faces to the Basin where the smoke of barbecue fires spirals among the Norfolk pines.

The shed on Bonnie Doon Wharf is the annual meeting spot of the Coasters Retreat Association. The minutes of the earliest meeting are dated 3 October 1948 and that meeting was held on Bennetts Wharf. Regular meetings lapsed until the 1950s. In keeping with the relaxed atmosphere of West Pittwater the Association meets every January on a pre-arranged

Sunday morning in the shed on the wharf. They then discuss any problems which may have arisen during the year.

As well as Audrey Shepherd's book on the area there is *Coaster's Retreat* by Jim Macken, published in 1991. The Hon. James Macken has been a barrister, lecturer and social commentator and a Judge of the New South Wales Industrial Commission. Another book is Sue Gould's *Pittwater Coasters Retreat: Recollections and Historical Notes,* published in 1994. A love for Pittwater, its history and pioneers emerges from these interesting books.

Right: 'A maid' brings the eggs, Bonnie Doon camp in the 1920's.

In earlier years people made their own entertainment. A mock beheading at a 1920s camp at Bonnie Doon at Coasters Retreat where the Alldritt family bought land in 1926.

The Basin

The regular ferry drops the holiday makers at the Basin but the area is also accessible to walkers via Ku-ring-gai Chase National Park along the 2.75 kilometre Basin Track. The track is a fire trail and passes heathland and a sheltered eucalypt forest down to the Basin. There is a wide variety of native flora, Aboriginal engravings, some tessellated pavement (patterned weathered rock surfaces) and near the end of the descent a wet sclerophyll forest of tall eucalypts.

The Basin is a popular camping spot. There is a Day Use Fee but children under five are free. The grassy flat is ideal for camping and the area is surrounded by wooded hills. A narrow channel connects the Basin to Pittwater.

It is a historic spot and was mentioned in Surveyor Larmer's survey of 1832. Robert McIntosh held 50 acres (20 hectares) of land here in 1835. In 1881 Frederick James Jackson acquired the Basin. A wealthy insurance broker Jackson was an early member of the Royal Prince Alfred Yacht Club. Jackson's estate was bought by the State Government of New South Wales in 1914 for £1250 and later included in Ku-ring-gai Chase. 'Sally' then became caretaker of the former Jackson home Beechwood for five shillings a week. Sally's yachting friends built a new cottage around Sally's old one and here she passed her final days. In 1916 a boatshed and bathing enclosure were completed and a new caretaker's cottage built in 1917. Repairs were then also carried out on Beechwood and it was used as a Trust Lodge.

Earlier in the late 1880s it was proposed defence installations should be installed at West Head and guns on Rock Head with troops stationed at the Basin.[115] Fortunately this idea never came to fruition as it would inevitably have spoiled the natural beauty of the Basin.

Summer and winter the Basin attracts holiday makers. Not far from the wharf is the memorial to Sally. There are tents beneath the Norfolk pines, the pines date from 1934, and people stroll along the beach. Youngsters build sand castles on the wet sand and others are 'messing about with boats'. Facilities once included a kiosk but the original toilet blocks and kiosk were removed by the National Park authorities. Now there are essential public facilities and a net enclosed swimming area. For many years Beacon Hill High School has used the area annually as a camp for Year 7 students to meet other students during an orientation period. There are bush walks and the vast area of Ku-ring-gai Chase to enjoy and on occasions Chase Alive Volunteers of the National Park show visitors around historic Beechwood House. The house has a heritage listing and was originally seven rooms with a shingle roof.

The ferry leaves the Basin Wharf and glides past high sandstone foreshores passing a small pristine beach opposite Coasters Retreat. Locally it is called Fisherman's Beach as local fishermen used to climb a rickety ladder built against a tree to look for schools of fish in the clear water. The beach has several local names.

There are towering cliffs and sandstone outcrops. Did unseen Aboriginal eyes gaze out at Governor Phillip's white intruders from here over two hundred years ago?

Currawong

Currawong is a private area owned by the Labor Council of New South Wales. Since 1950 they have owned nine cottages in the area and these are available to union members, and others, at reasonable rates.

Once Little Mackerel Beach, the area has a long history of private ownership. It was part of the land promised to John Clarke in 1823 and in the early 1830s Martin Burke received 100 acres (40 hectares), which he subsequently leased to Patrick Flynn. Burke had arrived in Sydney as a convict on the *Tellicherry* in 1806. He appears as a free settler aged 57 years in the 1828 Census. Apparently by 1885 there was litigation over the ownership of Little Mackerel Beach between the Wilson and Connell families and the tangled web of claimed ownership continued until 1886 when the Court finally decided that 60 acres (24 hectares) of Great Mackerel Beach go to a Gulargambone grazier, William Moore Connell. The Wilson family retained ownership of Little Mackerel Beach.[116] In 1872 Audrey Shepherd's great-great-grand-parents bought 40 acres (16 hectares) on Little Mackerel Beach.

In 1894 Ku-ring-gai Chase Trust was proclaimed and the trustees were alarmed at the prospect of the beaches being cut up into building allotments. The State Government, however, refused to acquire the land. In 1910 Little Mackerel Beach, some 48 acres (19 hectares), was purchased by Mrs. Stiles, wife of Dr. Bernard Stiles of Newtown. Here Dr. Stiles built a home, Midholme, and his son has early memories of the beach when it 'was an idyllic spot, the only private beach in all of Pittwater.'[117] Bernard Stiles recalls the lyrebirds, koalas and wallabies that frequented the spot. Wildflowers were thick at Little Mackerel Beach and on the Ku-ring-gai Plateau and the gullies of Little Mackerel provided turpentine timber. There is still turpentine within Ku-ring-gai Chase National Park behind Currawong.

Currawong remains an idyllic spot with timber cottages, coral trees, casuarinas and the clean white beach with views to Barrenjoey. From the beach there is a towering headland and folds of bush clad hillsides to Great Mackerel Beach.

Great Mackerel Beach

The local ferry enters the bay past the houses sheltering on the southern shore and ahead is the curving beach. Great Mackerel Beach is a small-scale, estuarine beach semi-protected from ocean waves. These western shore beaches exist because of the longshore drift of marine sand into the Pittwater estuary due to littoral currents generated by the penetration of ocean swell in the bay. If the 5 kilometre walk from West Head to Mackerel Beach is followed - it is rated as medium to difficult - there are superb views. Study the trees during the walk including the delightful blueberry ash. Its sprays of drooping white flowers are followed by bright blue berries. There are umbrella ferns, the common eggs and bacon *(Dillwynia retorta),* forest oak and coachwood. The views will constantly demand attention, the blue sweep of Pittwater and foreshores a world of sand, rocks and clear water. Nearing Mackerel Beach there is an open forest of red bloodwood and the track leads down eventually to the beach and lagoon.

Great Mackerel Beach is sheltered by high walls of rock and so is protected from the strong westerly winds. In the early days fishermen caught their bait here, hence the name Mackerel Beach. On Anniversary Day (now Australia Day - 26 January) 1920 Great Mackerel Beach was auctioned by H.W. Horning & Co. Ltd. The company produced a prospectus entitled Great Mackarel (sic) Beach, Ku-ring-gai Chase, Pittwater. It describes the area as one mile (1.6 km) across the water from Palm Beach, where there is a beach of 'semi-circular clean, white sand', an extensive flat, clumps of oak and 'the still waters of a picturesque lagoon'. The brochure continues 'There amidst alternate sunshine and shadow tracks radiate in all directions through scenes of sylvan loveliness'. It boasts boating, bathing and fishing; 'Like Balmoral and North Harbour it is a semi-surf beach, with hard, white sand glistening beneath the water...'. It also mentions 'the unchartered graves of two early settlers, a man and his wife, the foundations of whose ruined homestead may still be traced on one of the delightful knolls, whilst legend has it that a large sum in gold - presumably the result of their life savings - lies buried beside them.' This information was quoted in the brochure from the *Sun* 12 October 1918. Recently following a storm and flood the grave of a child was found and reburied, but, apparently, no pot of gold. The firm's brochure also quotes Ku-ring-gai Shire Council President, Councillor Fitzsimmons: 'This magnificent

sandy beach, inherently part and parcel of Ku-ring-gai Chase, ought never to have passed into private hands.' It further mentions the Chase's plea to the Minister for Lands to resume or purchase 'Big Mackerel Beach'.[118] At the time of the request by the Chase Trustees Great Mackerel Beach was owned by E. Blackwell.

The houses of Great Mackerel Beach are bathed in sunshine and several pelicans float on the bay. There are coral trees and boats pulled onto the beach. No doubt the residents are very glad the Minister for Lands did not accede to the request of the Ku-ring-gai Chase Trustees for the area is a little piece of paradise.

In 1967 a $70,000 electricity extension via submarine cable from Palm Beach brought power and light to Coasters Retreat, Currawong and Great Mackerel Beach on the western foreshores of Pittwater. On a soft night across the pewter coloured water the lights twinkle around these western settlements. However Great Mackerel Beach has no water supply, sewer or shops. Supplies are brought across from Palm Beach and even the local garbage has to be shipped across the water for collection at Palm Beach.

Great Mackerel Beach is part of Sydney and yet quite apart from Sydney and its sprawling suburbs. It retains the 'sylvan loveliness' noted in 1920. The ferry departs from the wharf carrying residents across to the mainland leaving the gentle ripple of wake across the waters of Pittwater.

Resolute Beach

Between Great Mackerel Beach and West Head lies Resolute Beach nestled among the headlands. In 1961 it was proposed that the National Fitness Camp be moved from West Head to the headland between the two beaches. Some 30

acres (12 hectares) was to be set aside for the camp and the Ku-ring-gai Chase Trust was initially prepared to offer 5 acres (2 hectares) on permissive occupancy. However they changed their minds and then opposed the proposed camp. The camp on West Head closed on 19 May 1964 and West Head was then developed with the resurfaced West Head Road, picnic area and information centre for the benefit of the public.

From West Head runs Resolute Track, 2 kilometres, starting from the Garigal picnic area. Near Resolute Beach there is a thick vegetation with handsome flatpea and native holly enjoying the moist and humid area. It is possible to make your way down to Resolute Beach. The view is to Barrenjoey Beach, the headland and lighthouse.

Ku-ring-gai Chase National Park and West Head

Looming behind all the western Pittwater settlements is Ku-ring-gai Chase National Park culminating in the glorious and breathtaking headland area of West Head.

The National Park is named for the Guringai people who lived on Hornsby Plateau. The park includes large outcrops of flat sandstone where the Aborigines engraved their rock carvings and made paintings in caves and overhangs. It is not surprising with the sea and Pittwater part of their life that many rock carvings feature fish and sometimes whales. The middens of discarded shellfish remains were plundered by the early white shell gatherers for lime supplies. The Aboriginal rock carvings are an important feature of Ku-ring-gai Chase National Park and may be observed on many of the area's attractive bush walks.

Ku-ring-gai Chase National Park covers 14,712 hectares and was established through the efforts of Eccleston Du Faur (1832-1915). Du Faur was London born in 1832 and educated at Harrow. In 1853 he emigrated to Victoria, later returning to England but again coming to

A tranquil view over the Pittwater/Hawkesbury area.

Australia as a draftsman to the Department of Lands in Sydney in 1863. With a partner he later became a pastoral agent. Du Faur had a keen interest in geography and led an expedition to look for explorer Ludwig Leichhardt. His interests were varied and he helped found the New South Wales Geographical Society and the Academy of Art in Sydney, the forerunner of the National Art Gallery of New South Wales.

Interested in his adopted land's flora and fauna, Du Faur saw the need for a national park on Sydney's northern boundary as the neighbourhood increased rapidly and there was subsequent destruction of bush and native plants. He owned a house, Flowton, built in 1895, at North Turramurra, now the administration block of the Lady Davidson Hospital. Du Faur invited the governor of the day, the Earl of Jersey, to visit the area and despite a prior ruling by the Department of Lands in 1891 that no further land was available for national parks an area of 35,000 acres (14 sq. kms) was dedicated as a reserve for public recreation in December 1894. It was controlled by nine trustees with Henry Copeland as President and Eccleston Du Faur as Managing Trustee. Copeland named the reserve Ku-ring-gai for the lost Aboriginal people and selected the word 'chase' meaning 'unenclosed park'. Du Faur became involved with Ku-ring-gai Chase, carried out surveys and laid roads and paths.

Ku-ring-gai Chase National Park has superb water views and more than 45 walking tracks. West Head on Pittwater is surrounded by deep waters, stunning scenery, a winding shoreline with sheltered anchorages for yachts and numerous well defined bush tracks.

Just past the Duck Hole near McCarrs Creek is an entrance to the Chase and West Head Road. Even from the roadway the bush tracks are clearly identifiable and marked. Each is a discovery walk.

Ponder on the Aboriginal carvings, wonder at the expanse of tessellated pavement, a curious sandstone formation where the rock is divided into small square blocks resembling mosaics caused by weathering of the weakest lines of sedimentary rock when it dried out and shrank. The weathering occurred at a faster rate along the faults because of the constant moisture within them. There are sticky sun-dews beside the tracks awaiting unsuspecting insects. Note the scribbly gums (Eucalyptus haemastoma) with their distinctive bark created by insect larvae eating under the bark, also angophora, banksias, tea tree, drumsticks, grevilleas and native fuchsia. There is the distant sweep of blue hills and the sounds of birds in the dense bush. To the left of the road heading to West Head lies Cowan Water. What an impression that vast area of peaceful water must have made on early explorers. The western area of the national park is linked to the timber getters of the upper North Shore for there were fine stands of Sydney blue gum, blackbutt, red cedar, coachwood and turpentine. From the 1830s the saw miller's rough camps crept along the North Shore while the settlers of Pittwater clung to their fertile areas.

The Lambert Peninsula and Commodore Heights recall Commodore Lambert who was Captain of HMS *Challenger* which visited Broken Bay between 1866 and 1870. Earlier, in 1834, 640 acres (260 hectares) of Commodore Heights was granted to explorer William Lawson (1774-1850) who crossed the Blue Mountains in 1813 with Gregory Blaxland and William Charles Wentworth. The land extended from West Head to Flint and Steel Point. Following the crossing of the mountains Lawson was granted 1000 acres (405 hectares) of land at Bathurst and became Commandant at Bathurst but resigned in 1824 and retired to his property at Prospect. The land at West Head is referred to in

Larmer's survey of 1832 as 'recently selected' although Lawson's grant is two years later. This area was not included in the area of the original Ku-ring-gai Chase but was offered to the Chase Trustees in 1911 at £1 per acre. This offer was not accepted and it was not until 1951 that West Head was included in Ku-ring-gai Chase. In 1967 the area of Ku-ring-gai Chase was put under the control of the National Parks and Wildlife Service.

West Head has survived as a glorious area of the National Park although at one time just prior to World War II a syndicate was raising money to establish a golf course on what had in colonial times been the Lawson grant. However with the declaration of war Sydney's defence was of prime importance and in 1940 50 acres (20 hectares) at West Head was utilised for defence purposes. Lawson's 640 acres (260 hectares) were also resumed and defence installations installed at West Head.

Concrete gun emplacements were installed at water level, with observation posts and search light positions. Equipment was lowered down the headland by a haulage line built of railway sleepers. A tramline joined the water-line gun sites. At the top of West Head a military camp was established. Included in the defences was a station for the detection of submarines by means of an underwater sonar loop between Barrenjoey and Box Head. Like Port Jackson at Sydney an anti-submarine net was located between Barrenjoey and West Head. In those dark days of the war the area bristled with anti-aircraft batteries. In 1942-1943 at Refuge Bay there was a secret training camp for 'Z Force' to raid Singapore Harbour. The famous *Krait*, now at the Australian National Maritime Museum at Darling Harbour, played an important role in this mission. Prior to World War II the *Krait* was a Japanese fishing boat operating from Singapore and named *Kofubu*

Maru. Following the bombing of Pearl Harbour and the Japanese invasion of Malaya the vessel was taken over by the Royal Navy in Singapore and following the fall of that city on 15 February 1942 the *Krait* was used by Australian Bill Reynolds to rescue escapees from Singapore. It is fitting that the *Krait* is now berthed at the Australian National Maritime Museum. A television series was made of the crew's exploits and for those who wish to read more of the story of the full operations of the *Krait* there is *The Heroes* by Ronald McKie published by Angus and Robertson, Sydney.

Today, where the military camp existed and searchlights probed the night skies, there is peace and beauty. Bird calls greet the visitor to West Head - the unique cry of the magpies, the laughter of the kookaburra and from the West Head Lookout, opened in 1965, there is a staggering view of Barrenjoey, Pittwater and Broken Bay. A myriad of blues encircle Lion Island which lies in Broken Bay, watching and waiting like the lions of Mycenae in ancient Greece. The island covers 8.9 hectares and rises to just over 86 metres. It was named Elliot Island by Governor Phillip. Phillip's friend, General Elliot, defeated the French and Spanish fleets at Gibraltar and it is believed Phillip saw a resemblance to Gibraltar in the island. Since 1933 Lion Island has been a reserve and it is a refuge for wild life including fairy penguins.

In the distance the view is to Patonga, Brisbane Water National Park and the line of northern headlands, beaches of yellow sand with white breakers crashing on sharp headlands. Again it is a blue and white world with the sails of the yachts small white triangles on a wash of deep blue. Across to Barrenjoey and the Palm Beach peninsula the view is enthralling, the sandstone lighthouse is a landmark. The view encompasses Palm Beach, its houses and moored vessels and sweeps around to Pittwater. Blue, green, white, the houses splashed amongst the bush like coloured daubs of paint on a canvas, the deep shadows on the hills and the clouds rolling in from the sea. The boats at Snapperman Beach, Palm Beach and Careel Bay are clearly discernible, like little balls of cotton wool stuck along the shore line continuing from Stripe Point to Taylors Point. On a winter's day the scene is one of clarity and gentle water.

This is an ancient area. It is near the centre of a large sedimentary basin, the Sydney Basin, developed during the Permian and Triassic periods. The rocks of the Lambert Peninsula and West Head are mostly sandstone with some shales. There is also evidence of volcanic action at West Head. The National Park includes the feature of 'flooded' or 'drowned' valleys. During the series of Ice Ages over the last million years sea levels were lower. Streams eroded valleys and when the ice caps melted the sea level rose and flooded the eroded valleys creating in this area Pittwater, Cowan Creek and Broken Bay. The last major rise of the sea level is believed to have occurred about 10000 years ago. Prominent hills such as today's Barrenjoey and Lion Island were then left isolated.

The Sydney sandstone has determined the landscape and its plant and animal life. Sandstone is composed of sand grains worn from rocks, weathered and carried by wind and water until accumulated in parallel layers and welded into the firm, granular stone. The striking feature of sandstone is the colour range caused by the sand grains and the nature of the natural cement which welds the stone together. There are various compounds such as iron oxide, calcium carbonate and silica. The sandstone may be white, grey, yellow/ochre, tan/red, rust or charcoal. Old exposed rock is often grey, covered with algae and lichen. Weathering causes interesting and fantastic sculpture to the sandstone, sometimes a honeycomb effect. Within Ku-ring-gai Chase National Park there are rock overhangs and caves, some evident along the walking tracks. The typical plants of the national park are heath, scrub, woodlands and open forest. Winter and spring are the best times to observe the prolific species of wildflowers within the park. Many have hard and prickly leaves and woody fruit, such as the hakea or needle bush, evolved for survival and renewal of growth after fire. There are the softer varieties of the purple boronia and the pink wax flower (Eriostemon lanceolatus). Over 800 plant species have been recorded in the national park area. The flowers attract honey-eaters and small marsupials. Some of the animals are nocturnal and shy and unlikely to be encountered although in early morning a wallaby may bound across the road and a sleepy possum has been found at midday curled up in a covered rubbish bin. Kookaburras and currawongs are both seen and heard and there are rosellas, wrens, the sulphur crested cockatoo with its screeching call and the honey-eaters with probing bill to seek out nectar. May to June is the mating season of the lyrebirds and they may be glimpsed at West Head and Garigal. Goannas, geckoes, skinks, bush rats, snakes and spiny ant-eaters may be encountered along a bush track.

At weekends the park is popular but it is quiet on weekdays. It is a perfect location for bush walking, sight seeing, picnicking, boating and camping. Near the Garigal picnic area there are the geological formation of dykes and diatremes of volcanic rock formed 160 million years ago. For those interested in the Aboriginal sites the oldest of these within the park pre-date the pyramids of Egypt and the Acropolis of Athens. As well as the rock engravings and cave drawings there are axe grinding grooves and the middens composed of shells, fire charcoal and some animal bones found near caves or river foreshores where the Aborigines feasted on oysters, mussels and shellfish.

The National Parks and Wildlife Service provides Chase Alive, a programme of guided walks and nature activities conducted by volunteer guides. There are night time walks to discover shy nocturnal creatures, bird walks and early morning chorus strolls, walks to the park's more spectacular lookouts, canoe safaris and visits to Aboriginal sites. Historical walks are also conducted to Barrenjoey Headland and marine tours to Long Reef near Collaroy.

Located only 24 kilometres from the centre of Sydney, Ku-ring-gai Chase National Park is Australia's second oldest national park, dedicated in 1894. Royal National Park is Australia's oldest park, established 1879, and is the world's second oldest national park after Yellowstone in the United States of America.

Pittwater Playground

Surveyor Govett in 1829 foresaw Pittwater, as quoted previously, as the site of 'ornamental villas of the rich and all these silent waters in times to come' resounding with 'the festivities of the merry and the gay.'[119]

The Aborigines must have enjoyed the advantages of Pittwater and even the early shellgatherers, fishing folk and timber getters were surely not unmindful of its beauty and natural attractions. Once settlers had established homes and families around Pittwater the children scrambled over rocks, played on the beaches, explored the bush, fished and gathered shellfish. Many of the families who later built homes or week-enders around Pittwater often came at first as campers to the area and there were favourite picnic spots on Pittwater.

Pittwater, perhaps, has not really changed all that much. Residents and visitors still enjoy its many attractions. There are the golf courses, tennis courts, swimming enclosures at the Basin, Paradise Beach and Taylors Point and the usual sporting activities offered in suburban areas. Pittwater also has its beaches, many quiet and secluded foreshore parks and picnic spots or the more remote enticing areas of West Pittwater. Ku-ring-gai Chase National Park offers a whole range of bush walks, views, bush picnic and barbecue sites and organised bush walks and activities.

But the waters of Pittwater are a playground too. Apart from swimming, there is wind surfing, diving and for those not skilled at certain activities there are schools such as the Barrenjoey Sailboard and Catamaran School & Hire at Palm Beach. The Scotland Island Sailing School offers lessons in yachting from beginners to advanced AYF certificate.

A wonderful way to relax is to enjoy our waterways, indulge perhaps in a little fishing, discover tiny clear beaches or lunch at one of the many restaurants and enjoy the beauty of Pittwater.

Some prefer to join a yacht club and Pittwater has several famous clubs. After the arrival of the Royal Prince Alfred Yacht Club camps were held at the Basin. The Easter Camp in 1900 attracted many yachtsmen including the Club's Commodore Samuel Hordern and his steam yacht *Bronzewing*. The yachtsmen had camps and marquees at the Basin, where they enjoyed fishing, good meals, sports and a concert. The yachts were decorated with coloured bunting and were illuminated at night by Chinese lanterns and lights.

In 1906 the Basin Cup was sailed from Port Jackson to Broken Bay and back. The 16 foot (4.8

A drawing from the Yachting Monthly by C. Fleming Williams entitled 'A Dinghy May Sometimes Be Of More Importance Than A 30-Tonner!'

Opposite Page: Pittwater Regatta on the second day of January 1924 was a day to dress up.

the season those normally participating in the Pittwater Regatta would enjoy the Christmas break. At the instigation of the Yachting Association of New South Wales there was some endeavour to resume the Pittwater Regatta but it never eventuated.

There are, however, club races on Pittwater. Some are annual events such as the Bayview Yacht Racing Association's marathon race. In 1992 51 centreboard yachts and eight keel boats participated and $700 was raised for the Peter Loft Memorial Foundation. The foundation helps young sailors participating in national and international events.

The old yachtsmen of Pittwater would be proud of the fact that for the Barcelona Olympic Games in 1992 almost half of the Australian yachting team hailed from Pittwater. The five Pittwater members were Glenn Bourke, Colin Beashel and Michael Mottl from the Royal Prince Alfred Yacht Club and Mitch Booth and John Forbes, Tornado cat world champions, from the Pittwater Catamaran Club. Booth and Forbes have been sailing Olympic class cats for over ten years. They have won four Australian and eight New South Wales titles. There were celebrations on Pittwater on 4 August 1992 when Booth and Forbes won the Bronze Medal at the Olympics. They had a dramatic finish in the Tornado catamaran event and completed the seven-race series only ten seconds away from gold. They are now planning to compete at the 1996 Atlanta Olympics. Avalon boatbuilder Colin Beashel was attending his third Olympics at Barcelona. He was a crew member of Australia Two in 1983 when the yacht won the America's Cup. Michael Mottl, from Scotland Island, was a member of Australia's Soling three-handed Keel boat crew at the Games.

For those less experienced than the Olympic sailors it is well to remember there are rules for those enjoying our waterways. The Maritime Services Board

metre) skiffs raced around Lion Island and this event was the first effort by the Royal Prince Alfred Yacht Club to organise regular racing for local yachtsmen. Because of the popularity of the event a public meeting was held and it was decided to hold a regatta. The first Pittwater Regatta was held on 16 March 1907. There were five sailing events, six rowing events in heavy skiffs and a race for motor launches. The Regatta was successful and it was then held annually until 1979 but had been disbanded during the two world wars. In 1980 the Pittwater Regatta Committee met and decided not to continue the regatta that year. The regatta had been held during the Christmas holiday period and it was felt that as there were enough races during

Waterways Authority warns against boating and drinking. New South Wales Police officers have been given power to test boaters for blood alcohol content. The Authority further warns of the necessity for carrying the correct lighting at night. During night time patrols the Authority stopped offenders endangering their own lives and other people by driving unlit boats. 'How many people would think of driving a car at night without lights?'[120]

Broken Bay Water Police in 1991 made 228 sea rescues and 383 in closed waters. Established in 1966 the Broken Bay Water Police also cope with thefts of, and from vessels, boating complaints, hoodlums, fires, illegal fishing, missing persons and drownings. The service patrols from Norah Head to Long Reef and 200 miles seawards. The police also conduct Young Adult Seamanship Training Programmes.

Inevitably pollution occurs on Pittwater and the Maritime Services Board conducts clean ups. The harbour cleaning fleet in 1992 had three vessels and a crew of twelve. The Pittwater Protection and Preservation Society supplied a list of sites to be cleaned and the clean-up boats recovered more than 50 tonnes of rubbish, including fallen trees, sunken boats and old pontoons.

Fishing

Since the early days Pittwater has been a favourite fishing spot and once also popular for oystering. Although in the 1850s the Hawkesbury was the favoured spot as it was felt the fishing in Pittwater was not as good because of the shallow waters and the presence of sharks.

Nowadays the whole Pittwater peninsula attracts those who enjoy fishing. On Pittwater there may be rock and weed close to the shore and many prefer to fish from a boat. There are numerous hire boat facilities around Pittwater. It is said the best time to catch the fish is two hours before high tide. A wide variety of fish may be caught around Pittwater including bream, flathead, jewfish, hairtail, whiting and blue swimmer crabs. On occasions hairtail is caught off Portuguese Beach with live bait of yellowtail or whole pilchards rigged on wire. Also around the peninsula area there are sea mullet, flounder, snapper, black bream, kingfish, drummer, rock cod, teraglin, trevally, gurnard and, of course, sharks.

Despite environmental problems the Hawkesbury River (recent tests show the Hawkesbury more polluted than India's Ganges) is productive and Brisbane Water across Broken Bay is said to be excellent. Pittwater is a little less constant fishwise than Brisbane Water.

It is sometimes asked where the fish go in winter but in August there are still bream in the Hawkesbury and blackfish may be caught in Pittwater. It is a case of knowledge and being in the right place at the right time.

Pittwater's Writers and Artists

Pittwater has long attracted writers and artists. Even in its early history the district so impressed visitors they were moved to record their impressions. One was Charles de Boos who walked from Manly to Palm Beach with two companions and a dog. His story is the subject of Guy Jennings' *My Holiday and Other Early Travels from Manly to Palm Beach*.

Writers, both past and present, proliferate around Pittwater.

Narrabeen is now part of the

Municipality of Pittwater and was visited by D.H. Lawrence (1885-1930) in 1922. He used the location in his novel *Kangaroo*. Frank Hardy (1917-1994), author of *Power Without Glory* (which resulted in the author being charged with criminal libel) once lived in Powderworks Road, Narrabeen. He used the incidents from a strike by Warringah Shire Council workers as the basis for his book *The Outcasts of Foolgarah*. Richard (Dick) Edwards, one time Chairman of the New South Wales Publications Classification Board, writer and poet has lived at various locations on the northern peninsula including Elanora.

In the 1930s Ion Idriess (1889-1979) had great success with *Lasseter's Last Ride* (84,000 copies sold) and *Flynn of the Inland* (84,000 copies) and by 1955 had published 42 books with a total sale of 1,500,000 copies. Ion Idriess died at Mona Vale on 6 June 1979. Austrian-born Rudi Krawsmann, poet, tutor and broadcaster is a Pittwater resident and features Mona Vale in *Waree*.

Newport was where poet Chris Brennan (1870-1932) chose to live for a number of years. Brennan purchased land near Bungan Head about 1903 and visited at weekends. He later came to live in the district in 1917 with his wife, Anna Werth. After the break up of their marriage Brennan left in 1923 and subsequently resided at Paddington. Children's author Allan Baillie (1943 -) also lives at Newport. He won the Kathleen Fidler Award in 1983 for his novel *Adrift*. Colleen Klein was born in Blacktown and when she came to Newport in the 1950s thought she had 'been set down in Paradise.'[121] Rowan Hewison (1949 -) resides overseas but was born in Newport and his novel *Salt Pan* (1980) is semi-autobiographical and set in the 1950s around Pittwater.

Bilgola has several literary connections. Poet Grace Perry (1927-1987) lived here and was often visited by members of the Poetry Australia Society, including James Dickey and Andrei Voznesensky. Perry later moved to a lovely old home at Berrima but retained the Bilgola property as a second home. Thomas Keneally (1935-) moved to Bilgola from Clareville. The suburb is featured in his novel *Passenger* (1979) where he mentions a house, the window 'touched by the first diffused gold of a sun that had travelled from Peru.' Iain Finlay and Trish Sheppard reside at Bilgola and jointly wrote *Africa Overland* (1977) and *South America Overland* (1980). Both have written separate works. The son of early politician William Bede Dalley, John Bede Dalley (1876-1935) also lived at Bilgola. He wrote satirical novels and is believed to have drowned while rock fishing at Bilgola on 6 September 1935. Prolific author Morris West (1916-) lived for many years overseas but returned to Australia and now lives at Bilgola.

Avalon was the home of Frank Clune, who lived at 28 Ruskin Row, which included its own small rainforest. Clune was the author of a large number of works including Australian history *Wild Colonial Boys* (1948) and *The Kelly Hunters* (1954); adventure stories; biography; exploration; historical novels and travel. His autobiographies are *Try Anything Once* and *Try Anything Twice*. English-born Alan Sharpe knew he had discovered the perfect spot when he first visited the peninsula. Sharpe lives in Avalon and is the author of *Pictorial Memories - Manly to Palm Beach* and other historical works.

Amy Mack (c.1877-1939) author of the delightful *A Bush Calendar* and other works used to holiday at Four Winds on Sunrise Hill at Palm Beach. Writer Nancy Phelan used to holiday with her aunt Amy Mack at Palm Beach. Born in Lismore, NSW, playwright

Bob Ellis (1942-) lives at Palm Beach.

Elanora Heights and Clareville are associated with Geoff Pike. In the 1950s he spent a year at Clareville and later built a house at Elanora Heights. He is the author of six books and his story *The Mangrove Man* is set around Pittwater. Journalist, writer and producer of feature films, Di Morrissey, spent her childhood at Lovett Bay on Pittwater and later lived at Mona Vale. She remembers a simple childhood coloured by a collection of 'eccentric and rich (thought not in the monetary sense) hotch-potch of characters.'[122]

Co-founder of the famous *Bulletin* J.F. Archibald (1856-1919) lived at Church Point for various periods between 1908-1910.

Across the water on Scotland Island is L.H. Evers, children's author. Poet, novelist and essayist James Cowan also lived on the island in the 1970s.

Pittwater's literary associations seem endless - poet Les Murray spent his honeymoon at Mona Vale and still visits Pittwater. Journaist/writer Phil Jarratt is the author of *Peninsularity*, a collection of essays about the northern penin-

sula. Peter Skrzynecki emigrated to Australia as a child and grew up in Sydney. The peninsula features in some of his poetry. Noela Young has written and illustrated four children's books as well as illustrating numerous other books. Her husband, Walter Cunningham, who died in 1988, was also a noted illustrator. Multi-talented Roy Fluke is both a poet, artist and sculptor. Rod Milgate, distinguished in both art and literature has been a noted Peninsula resident for many years. Peter Corris (1942-) uses the northern beaches area in several of his Cliff Hardy private detective books. Jean Dixon tells the story of gunpowder manufacturer Carl von Bieren in *The Riddle of Powderworks Road* (1980). Melbourne born Robert Drewe (1943-) has also used the northern beaches as a source of inspiration. The *Beach-Front Murders* (1985) by Tom Howard (1937-) is partly set in Palm Beach and Lion island. Dorothea Mackellar's (1885-1968) association with Lovett Bay has already been noted while Joan Phipson's novel *A Tide Flowing* (1981) features Avalon.

Artists

It is not surprising that a magnificent scenic area such as Pittwater has attracted artists. The first artists were the local Aborigines who used caves and flat rocks for their distinctive paintings and carvings. The First Fleet diarists included sketches of the area in their journals. Australian Impressionist Sydney Long visited a Bohemian hideaway at Newport in the 1890s and 1900s and Norman Lindsay was another visitor to the peninsula. The tradition of artists and Pittwater continues to the present day.

Arthur Murch (1902-1991) lived for many years at Avalon and some of his sculptures were featured in his garden. While further along the same street Wendy Sharpe, the first woman to receive the coveted Sulman Art Prize in 32 years, spent part of her childhood. Robert Lovett has a long association with the area. He says 'its beauty and character has not been spoiled over the years.' Neville Cayley,[123] one of the world's outstanding bird painters, spent his last years here where he died in 1950. Elaine Haxton and her association with Clareville has been noted as has Sali Herman's family residency in the same suburb. Newton Hedstrom's family has a long connection with Narrabeen and his wife Marjory Penglase was also an artist. Roy Fluke's work is largely abstract and semi-abstract. Darcy Forden's home and studio overlooks Narrabeen. Rod Milgate is both writer and artist and winner of the Blake Prize. Graham Austin was a founding member of the Peninsula Art Society in 1981. Both Noreen Gibson Fort and Sidney Fort were also foundation members of the same society. Maud Kemp has also lived in the area for many years and initiated the formation of the Peninsula Art Society. Polish born Stan Teliga is represented in the Australian National Gallery, state and regional galleries and lives at Bayview. Allan Waite lives in Harbord but many of his paintings feature Pittwater. Another foundation member of the Peninsula Art Society is Bob Baird and his work too features local areas. Judith White was well known with her art school at Narrabeen and in 1988 continued her studies in Venice and London. Dianne Ogg is another Peninsula artist. Dianne trained at the Julian Ashton School and the Royal Art Society and has won a number of local awards. Clem Seale

enjoyed a long career in art and produced thousands of black and white drawings. Many of the artists, including Pamela Thalben-Ball have selected local views or features for their work. Roderick Shaw attended Manly Public School and since World War II has chosen to live above Narrabeen Lagoon. Robyn Culley is a resident of Scotland Island. Paul Smith, another resident of Scotland Island acknowledges the island has influenced his work. Fabia Tory has also been inspired by Scotland Island in her art.

Master photographer Max Dupain, who died in July 1992, had a holiday house at Newport and took many photographs around the northern beaches. No doubt Pittwater will always attract writers and artists.

Architects too have found inspiration here including Canberra's designer Walter Burley Griffin who built a lodge at 35 Plateau Road, Avalon. Owned by the National Trust of Australia (NSW), the Lodge received a $150,000 heritage grant in 1992.

The rich and famous have also discovered Pittwater's charms, including Dame Joan Sutherland and husband Richard Bonynge, socialite Susan Renouf and actors Brian Brown and Rachel Ward.[124]

Pittwater Municipal Council

May 1, 1992 was constitution day for Pittwater Municipal Council when Warringah Shire Council's A Riding ceased to exist and the new municipality was born.

There had been a community struggle for independent local government for almost three decades. The Local Government Minister, Gerry Peacocke, approved the secession of Pittwater following an overwhelming Yes vote by A riding residents in a poll conducted in

1991. The secession by popular demand of a local government area was the first in New South Wales for almost 100 years and Pittwater became the first new local government area to be created since Lane Cove 97 years earlier.

The provisional council was made up of three elected members, and six appointees (three for their professional background, three for their community background). Following the Council's first election the Council is now composed of three wards with three elected councillors in each ward. The council seeks to balance the needs of a strong conservation ethic with desirable developments that do not over-tax community resources such as car parking space, access to foreshores and bushland and the maintenance of a quality lifestyle.

The headquarters of Pittwater Council are at 5 Vuko Place, Warriewood. The late Eric Green became the first mayor. The logo for the new council was designed by Hugh Seelenmeyer, a resident of Bushrangers Hill, Newport and the logo represents the peninsula as a place of water surrounded by trees.

Clareville Wharf on Pittwater, near Avalon.

eville wharf, Pittwater near Avalon Beach

Activity around Gonsalves boatshed
c. 1940.

*Gonsalves boat shed when it
operated as a store.*

Bibliography

Baglin, Douglas & Austin Yvonne, *Sydney Sandstone*, Rigby, 1976.

Berzins, Baiba, *The Coming of the Strangers - Life in Australia 1788-1822*, Collins Australia in association with the State Library of New South Wales, 1988.

Bradley, Lieutenant William, *A Voyage to New South Wales, 1786-1792*. Public Library of New South Wales with Ure Smith Pty. Ltd., 1969.

Burnum Burnum's Aboriginal Australia - A Traveller's Guide. Angus & Robertson, 1988.

Chisholm, Alec, (Editor) John White, *Journal of A Voyage to New South Wales*. Angus & Robertson, 1962.

Corbett, Alan, *Church Point and McCarr's Creek - A Nostalgic Look at the Past*. Edited, designed and produced by Claudette Moffatt.

Encyclopedia Britannica.

Fairley, Alan, *The Beaten Track - A Guide to the Bushland Around Sydney*. 1972.

Fairley, Alan, *Along The Track - A Guide to the Bushland Around Sydney*. 1974.

Fitzgerald, Shirley & Keating, Christopher, *Millers Point - The Urban Village*. Hale & Iremonger, 1991.

Geological Excursion guide to the seacliffs north of Sydney, University of New England, 1976.

Historical Records of Australia.

Hunter, Captain John, *An historical journal of events at Sydney and at sea - 1789-1792*. Angus & Robertson, 1968.

Jennings, Guy, *The Newport Story*. Guy Jennings, 1987.

Jennings, Guy, *My Holiday and other early travels from Manly to Palm Beach 1861*. Aramo Pty. Ltd., Newport Beach, 1991.

Journal, Royal Australian Historical Society, No. 26, 1940.

Journal, Royal Australian Historical Society, No. VI, 1920.

Journal, Church of England Historical Society, Vol.4, No.2, June, 1959.

Lawrence, Joan, *Sydney from The Rocks*. Hale & Iremonger, 1988.

Lawrence, Joan, *North Shore Walks*. Hale & Iremonger, 1991.

Macken, Jim, *Coasters' Retreat*. James J. Macken, 1991.

Manly Warringah Journal of Local History, Vol.1, No.4, 'Governor Phillip and Companions in Manly Warringah'.

Norman, Graeme, *Yachting and the Royal Prince Alfred Yacht Club*. Child & Associates, French's Forest, NSW, 1988.

Park, Ruth, *The Companion Guide to Sydney*. Collins, 1973.

Pollon, Frances, *The Book of Sydney Suburbs*. Angus & Robertson, 1988.

Prentis, Malcolm D., (ed.), *Warringah History*, Warringah Shire Council, 1988.

Sharpe, Alan, *Pictorial Memories: Manly to Palm Beach*. Atrand, 1983.

Shepherd, Audrey, *The Halcyon Days of Summer on Pittwater - 150 Years of Settlement at Coaster's Retreat. 1842-1992*. Published by Audrey Shepherd, Middle, Cove, NSW, 1992.

Smith, P. & J., Ecological Consultants, 'Draft Angophora Reserve and Hudson Park, Plan of Management', Warringah Shire Council, February, 1992.

Steege, Joan (ed.), *Palm Beach 1788-1988*. The Palm Beach Association, 1988.

Taylor, Professor Griffith, *Sydneyside Scenery*. Angus & Robertson, 1958.

Tindale, N.B., *Aboriginal Tribes of Australia*. ANU, Canberra, 1974.

Turbet, Peter, *The Aborigines of the Sydney District Before 1788*. Kangaroo Press, 1989.

Warringah 1988 - A Celebration by its Artists and Writers. Warringah Shire Council, 1988.

Footnotes

1 Sparks, Jervis, *Tales From Barranjoey,* Jervis Sparks, 1992.

2 Chisholm, Alec H. (ed.), *Journal of a Voyage to New South Wales,* Surgeon John White Angus & Robertson, 1962.

3 Flower, Cedric, *Duck and Cabbage Tree - A Pictorial History of Clothes in Australia, 1788-1914,* Angus and Robertson, 1968.

4 Hunter, Captain John, *An Historical Journal of Events at Sydney and at Sea, 1787-1792* Angus & Robertson, 1968.

5 Cobley, John, *Sydney Cove, 1789-1790* Angus & Robertson, Sydney, 1963.

6 Tindale, N.B., *Aboriginal Tribes of Australia* ANU, Canberra, 1974.

7 *Burnum Burnum's Aboriginal Australia - A Traveller's Guide* Angus & Robertson, 1988.

8 Worgan, George B. *Journal of a First Fleet Surgeon,* Library Council of N.S.W., Sydney, 1978.

9 Dispatch of Governor Phillip to Lord Sydney dated 15 May 1788.

10 *A Voyage to New South Wales, The Journal of Lieutenant William Bradley, of HMS Sirius, 1786-1792,* Facsimile, Mitchell Library, Public Library of New South Wales with Ure Smith Pty. Ltd. 1969.

11 ibid.

12 ibid.

13 ibid.

14 Journal of a Voyage to New South Wales, by Surgeon John White.

15 ibid.

16 Berzins, Baiba in *The Coming of the Strangers - Life in Australia 1788 - 1822.* Collins Australia in association with the State Library of New South Wales. Berzins states 'It was not until 1791, on an expedition to Broken Bay, that the Europeans realised that the Aboriginals accompanying them spoke a different language to those they met in the area.'

17 Arabanoo was captured at Manly on Phillip's orders in an endeavour to establish relations between the Aborigines and settlers. He died of smallpox in 1789.

18 Hunter, Captain John, *An Historical Journal of Events at Sydney and at Sea, 1787-1792.* Angus & Robertson, 1968.

19 P.H. Curson in Times of Crisis (1985) suggests the epidemic may have been chickenpox as it killed few, if any, whites.

20 Tench, Captain W. *Sydney's First Four Years, A Narrative of an Expedition to Botany Bay, and a Complete Account of the Settlement at Port Jackson.* Angus & Robertson, 1961.

21 The spearing occurred on 7 September 1790. Bennelong was the most famous of the Aborigines captured by Phillip's orders.

22 Morris, Jan, *Sydney.* Viking, 1992.

23 Reprint of Journal of Captain James Cook, Mitchell Library, State Library of New South Wales.

24 Governor Phillip's dispatch to Lord Sydney 15 May 1788.

25 ibid.

26 Quoted in RAHS Journal Vol. VI, Part IV, 1920.

27 ibid.

28 ibid.

29 ibid.

30 ibid.

31 ibid.

32 *Sydney Morning Herald* 17 April 1880. State Library of New South Wales.

33 ibid.

34 ibid.

35 ibid.

36 ibid.

37 ibid.

38 Traditional Cornish smuggling song.

39 Sydney Customs Notice dated 6.8.1841.

40 Swancott, Charles, *The Brisbane Water Story,* Part 3.

41 RAHS Journal Vol. VI, Part IV, 1920.

42 Prentis, Martin D. (ed.), *Warringah History,* Warringah Shire Council, 1988.

43 Article supplied by Mike Buesnel, Atlantis Divers.

44 ibid.

45 ibid.

46 Information from *Pittwater Life,* Volume 2, No.1.

47 *RAHS Journal* Vol. VI, Part IV, 1920.

48 ibid.

49 ibid.

50 *RAHS Journal* Vol. VI, Part IV, 1920.

51 Swancott, Charles, *Dee Why to Barrenjoey and Pittwater,* D.S. Ford, Printers.

52 *RAHS Journal* Vol. VI, Part IV, 1920.

53 *My Holiday and other early travels from Manly to Palm Beach. 1861,* compiled by Guy Jennings. Aramo Pty. Ltd., 1991.

54 ibid.

55 Park, Ruth, *The Companion Guide to Sydney,* Collins, 1973.

56 Pollon, Frances, *The Book of Sydney Suburbs,* Angus & Robertson, 1988.

57 Kennedy, Brian & Barbara, *Sydney and Suburbs A History and Description,* Reed, 1982.

58 See *RAHS Journal,* Vol. VI, Part IV, 1920.

59 See Jennings, Guy, *The Newport Story,* 1987 for details of other grants P.10.

60 The Village Reserve covered 75 acres, bounded by Neptune Street in the south and the start of the Bilgola Bends in the north. See Jennings P.10.

61 Pittwater Lakes Album, 1880. Mitchell Library, State Library of New South Wales.

62 *RAHS Journal* Vol. VI, Part IV, 1920.

63 ibid.

64 Land Titles Office, S2, p.341.

65 Unnamed newspaper cutting, 1919. Mitchell Library, State Library of New South Wales.
66 Description of Newport. Pittwater and Hawkesbury Lakes, 1880, Mitchell Library, State Library of New South Wales.
67 *Sydney Morning Herald,* 17 April 1880.
68 Description of Newport. Pittwater and Hawkesbury Lakes, 1880, Mitchell Library, State Library of New South Wales.
69 Swancott, Charles, *Dee Why to Barrenjoey and Pittwater,* D.S. Ford, Printers.
70 1928 advertisement.
71 Norman, Graeme, *Yachting and the Royal Prince Alfred Yacht Club,* Child & Associates. 1988.
72 *RAHS Journal* No.26, 1940, P.326.
73 The exploratory party had left Manly on 22 August 1788 to examine the coast to Broken Bay.
74 Journal of a Voyage to New South Wales, by Surgeon John White.
75 *RAHS Journal* No. 26, 1940.
76 ibid.
77 Kalori School Magazine 1968.
78 ibid.
79 Swancott, Charles, Dee *Why to Barrenjoey and Pittwater,* D.S. Ford, Printers, P.25.
80 Quoted by J.S.N. Wheeler in *RAHS Journal* No. 26, 1940.
81 ibid.
82 *RAHS Journal* Vol. VI, Part IV, 1920.
83 Boyd, Robin, *The Australian Ugliness,* F.W. Cheshire, Melbourne, 1960.
84 *RAHS Journal,* No.26, 1940.
85 The National Trust of Australia (NSW) Activity Booklet, No. 427, Bayview, Sunday 23.9.1979. Mitchell Library, State Library of New South Wales.
86 ibid.
87 Quoted in Scotland Island News - March 21, 1992 - Vol. 32, No.1.
88 ibid.
89 Ryan, R.J., B.A., (Ed.), Land Grants 1788-1809, Australian Documents Library.
90 Gledhill, P.W., *Manly and Pittwater, Its Beauty and Progress.*
91 Letter from Macquarie to Lord Sidmouth quoted in *Lachlan Macquarie, His Life and Times,* M.H. Ellis, Angus and Robertson, 1947.
92 Macquarie Journal A778, Mitchell Library, State Library of New South Wales.
93 *Sydney Gazette* 24 November 1812, Mitchell Library, State Library of New South Wales.
94 *RAHS Journal* Vol. VI, Part IV, 1920.
95 Swancott, Charles, *Dee Why to Barrenjoey and Pittwater,* D.S. Ford, Printers.
96 *RAHS Journal* No.26, 1940.
97 Lester Warburton, Scotland Island.
98 ibid.
99 Karmel Patterson, Scotland Island Residents Association.
100 Gledhill, P.W., *Manly and Pittwater, Its Beauty and Progress.*
101 Gledhill, P.W., *Manly and Pittwater, Its Beauty and Progress.*
102 *RAHS Journal* No. 26,1940.
103 ibid.
104 Corbett, Alan, *Church Point and McCarr's Creek, a Nostalgic Look at the Past.* Claudette Moffatt.
105 ibid.
106 ibid.
107 *Warringah 1988 A Celebration by its Artists and Writers,* Warringah Shire Council, 1988.
108 Quoted in *Warringah 1988 - A Celebration by its Artists and Writers.*
109 'My Country' by Dorothy Mackellar.
110 Macken, Jim, *Coaster's Retreat.* James J. Macken, 1991.
111 ibid.
112 Caption to photograph on ferry Myra.
113 Shepherd, Audrey, *The Halcyon Days of Summer on Pittwater.* 150 Years of Settlement at Coaster's Retreat. 1842-1992. Middle Cove, NSW, 1991.
114 Published by H.W. Horning & Co. Ltd., 1920, Mitchell Library, State Library of New South Wales.
115 *RAHS Journal* Vol.VI, 1920, Part IV, P.189. Maybanke Anderson suggests Rock Head was a name for part of Coaster's Retreat.
116 *Shepherd, The Halcyon Days of Summer on Pittwater.* 150 Years of Settlement at Coaster's Retreat. 1842-1992. Pps. 45 & 46.
117 Macken, Jim, *Coaster's Retreat,* James J. Macken, 1991.
118 All quotes from Great Mackerel Beach, Ku-ring-gai Chase, Pittwater. H.W. Horning & Co. Ltd., Mitchell Library, State Library of New South Wales.
119 Journal of Surveyor W.M. Govett, Mitchell Library, State Library of New South Wales.
120 Michael Chapman, Maritime Services Board Waterways Authority.
121 *Warringah 1988 A Celebration by its Artists and Writers.* Warringah Shire Council. 1988.
122 *Warringah 1988 A Celebration by its Artists and Writers.*
123 *Warringah 1988 A Celebration by its Artists and Writers.*
124 Sources - *Warringah 1988 A Celebration by its Artists and Writers,* Warringah Shire Council, 1988. Pierce, Peter (ed.), *The Oxford Literary Guide to Australia.* OUP 1987. Australian Dictionary of Biography. Only writers and artists living in the new Municipality of Pittwater has been included.

Photograph Acknowledgements

T = top, M = middle, B = bottom

Alldritt family: 81T, 81B
Australia Post Historical Archives: 19
Carl and Caressa Gonsalves: 22, 25, 26T, 27, 28B, 29T, 29B, 32T, 32M, 32B, 33B, 34, 35, 77, 78, 90
Manly Waringah and Pittwater Historical Society: 15
Mitchell Library: 9, 10, 31B (Alen Album PXD591), 85 (Q951/G)
Royal Prince Alfred Yacht Club: 50, 51
Laurie Seaman: 4, 21, 23, 26B, 28T, 30B, 31T, 33T
Alan Sharpe: 41, 46, 47, 48, 49, 54, 55, 57T, 57B, 58, 61, 62, 63, 91, 96
Jervis Sparks: 13, 16, 18, 30T
Peter Verrills: 37T, 37B, 97, 98
Catherine Warne: 36

Index